SMALL GROUP
STUDENT
MANUAL

BIBLICAL FINANCIAL STUDY

CROWN FINANCIAL MINISTRIES

biblical financial freedom

Crownuk.org

Module study schedule

Study options

Biblical Financial Studies is a flexible, modular, programme with ten studies. This study is for everyone – single or married, young or old, whether you regard yourself as a high or low earner, rich or poor.

The study is structured so that it is easy to study as:

- an individual
- a couple or
- as a group member

How long will the study take?

The ten modules are structured so that each study takes a week. Thus, using the weekly approach the study will last ten weeks. Is it possible to complete the study in less than ten weeks? Yes, but before we suggest a number of study options, let us firstly explain the rationale behind the ten weeks. This course has many benefits other than financial and it does take time to gain full advantage and develop new habits. When we accept Christ as Saviour we are starting the journey of making Him Lord. Many people's finances are in need of alignment with the Word of God. Students around the world testify to the benefit they derive from the study; these benefits include:

- Developing a closer walk with the Lord
- Increasing their Bible study time
- Greater commitment to praying for people
- Reduction in debt
- Better financial skills
- Increased savings

In particular, where the group members do not know each other well, the ten weeks allow relationships to be birthed while others are deepened. So this financial study has an overflow!

However, we recognise that it is not always possible for a church to set aside ten weeks and so we include below a suggested combination of self and group study.

Four to eight week study groups

If you have elected to study this course with four to eight group meetings some of your study modules will be self-study. Your Crown leader will confirm the group plan and which modules are for self-study. For the self-study modules continue with the study as though it were in a group setting, learning the memory verse, completing the personal study and the practical application workbook. Your Crown leader will agree with the group their plans for dealing with any questions you may have regarding the self-study questions or the practical application workbook.

Please note that based on Crown's experience you will only derive the full benefit from studying this course with a group over the full ten weeks

Group study

Your Crown leader will run though the way in which a Crown study group works.

No.	Module	Four weeks	Six weeks	Eight weeks	Your group
1	Getting started				
2	God's part/our part	*	*	*	
3	Work	*	*	*	
4	Debt	*	*	*	
5	Counsel				
6	Lifestyle		*	*	
7	Honesty			*	
8	Giving	*	*	*	
9	Saving and investing		*	*	
10	Eternity			*	

Biblical financial study plan

* These are the recommended study modules. The weeks left blank represent the self-study modules.

And finally, if you are a single person, you will need to adapt the text to your circumstances where reference is made to a couple or spouse.

Introduction

We are pleased that you have decided to study Crown's Biblical Financial Study. God has used the principles you are about to learn in the lives of literally millions who have undertaken this study. This study is about finance, an area that impacts our everyday life. However, the study addresses areas that impact how we handle our finances including attitudes, commitments, values, lifestyle and all of this with an eye on our eventual destination – eternity.

There are a variety of study approaches you may adopt, depending on your circumstances. We outlined these on page iii. We have learned that people benefit most when they are faithful to complete the following:

Start by reading *Your Money Counts*. This book is easy to read and will provide you with a good overview of this study. Then, complete these requirements for each module:

1. Personal study

The study modules are structured on a weekly basis with about 15 minutes study every day. Each module comprises Bible verses followed by questions that relate to their application. Space is provided in the study manual for your responses to the questions. The questions are asked in such a way as to emphasise what you believe the Bible is saying and how this applies; they are not questions that ask you to be specific about your own financial position.

2. Scripture memory

Paul instructs us in Colossians 3:16 to *"let the word of Christ dwell in you richly"* while in Psalm 119:11 the psalmist says *"I have hidden your word in my heart that I might not sin against you."* In each module you will find a key memory verse. We encourage you to memorise each verse as this will help you remember the most important principles.

3. Practical application workbook

As you complete each module there is a practical financial exercise, such as beginning a budget or designing a debt repayment programme.

4. If you are studying this as a member of a group: pray for one another

Everyone prays for the other group members every day. Answers to prayers are one of the most encouraging results of the Crown study experience.

Group attendance

Everyone should attend at least eight of the 10 modular studies. Please let your leaders know in advance if you anticipate missing a meeting or arriving late. The meetings are planned to start and end on time.

My thanks to Howard Dayton, the co-founder of Crown, for his faithfulness in seeking God over the 30 years that this study has been in development. I am grateful to him for allowing me to adapt this study.

We trust you will be blessed as you participate in the Biblical Financial Study. We pray as we send out these study guides that the Lord will bless you in every way as you learn His financial principles.

Mark Lloydbottom, Co-author
Crown Financial Ministries: UK National Director

Purpose

The purpose of this Biblical Financial Study is to teach people God's financial principles in order to know Christ more intimately and to be free to serve Him

Financial policy

- Crown Financial Ministries does not endorse, recommend or sell any financial investments. No one may use affiliation with Crown to promote or influence the sale of any financial products or services.

- Crown's *Biblical Financial Study* does not give specific investment advice. No one may use his or her affiliation with Crown to give investment advice.

- This study is affordably priced because we do not want cost to be an obstacle to people who desire to participate. If you find the study valuable and want to help make it available to others, you may make a donation to Crown; please visit our website at www.crownuk.org.

Website

Crown has a website as a resource to provide study group members and leaders with up-to-date and detailed financial information based on what the Bible teaches about how we handle our money, debt, wealth and possessions. It contains helpful articles, a categorised list of the verses dealing with possessions, and links to other useful websites.

Visit the our website at Crownuk.org for a range of further information on our studies for churches, children and business owners. Here you will find a range of study materials and DVDs.

Register at www.crownuk.org

A critical ingredient of taking part in a Crown group study is what happens *after* the study. It is our desire to provide important and useful resources and information that will assist you as you walk in the principles you are learning in this study. For us to do this we need to know who you are and how to get this information to you.

Please take a moment and complete the student group form online in the "My Crown" section of Crownuk.org. When you enroll as a group member, you will have access to helpful tools and information to assist you during this study.

> **"Therefore if you have not been faithful in the use of worldly wealth, who will entrust the true riches to you?"**
> **(Luke 16:11, NASB)**

module one
Getting started

How we handle money impacts our relationship with the Lord

module one
Personal study

To be completed **prior to** module one meeting

Scripture to memorise
"Therefore if you have not been faithful in the use of worldly wealth, who will entrust the true riches to you?" (Luke 16:11, NASB)

Practical application
In addition to reading *Your Money Counts*, please memorise the Scripture above. In your practical application workbook please read the background notes to the spending tracker: start to complete the spending tracker and review your filing system. Please also register at My Crown at www.crownuk.org

---

Personal study

1. What did you learn from *Your Money Counts* that you found helpful?

Read Isaiah 55:8-9 and Romans 12:2

2. Based on this passage, do you think God's financial principles will differ from how most people handle money? What do you think would be the greatest difference?

God is in control of our economy. God economy is different to the world's system.

Read Luke 16:11

3. What does this verse communicate to you about the importance of managing possessions faithfully?

How you handle finances has a direct relationship with your relationship with Christ.

4. How does handling money impact our fellowship with the Lord?

Brings us close to God

Scripture memory helps
The memory verses are found on the card supplied with this study and are also available as a download from My Crown at Crownuk.org.

What is Crown's stance on...?

We are often asked this question. The study first asks the student to read the Personal Study each day and respond to the questions. This is the first stage in discovering what you believe the Bible has to say on a particular topic. Then when you meet with your Crown study group, you will hear from the other members, so that you develop an understanding of how others have responded. Finally, at the beginning of each module you will be asked to go back and read some helpful notes that we have prepared on the previous week's module. We have found that this approach works well and rightly ensures that there is a focus on what God's Word is revealing to you and your group. We trust you will find our insights helpful and a blessing.

If you are studying this in a ten-week Crown group then your first module is complete. All other students, please continue with the study.

module one
Crown notes

To be read after completing **module one** personal study

This study will transform your life and finances as you learn what the God of the universe says about handling money.

The way most people handle money is in sharp contrast to God's financial principles. Isaiah 55:8 says it this way *"for my thoughts are not your thoughts, neither are your ways my ways,' declares the Lord."* The most significant difference between the two is that the Bible reveals God is closely involved with our finances. Many people fail to realise it because He has chosen to be invisible to us and to operate in the unseen supernatural realm.

The Bible and money

It may surprise you to learn how much the Bible says about finances. More than 2,350 verses address God's way of handling money and possessions. Jesus Christ said more about money than almost any other subject, and He did so for three reasons.

1. How we handle money impacts our fellowship with God

Jesus equates how we handle our money with the quality of our spiritual life. In Luke 16:11 (TLB), He says *"and if you are untrustworthy about worldly wealth, who will trust you with the true riches of heaven?"* The true riches in life are a close relationship with the Lord.

If we handle money according to the principles of Scripture, we enjoy closer fellowship with Christ. The parable of the talents demonstrates this as the master congratulates the servant who managed his money faithfully: *"Well done, good and faithful servant! You have been faithful with a few things; I will put you in charge of many things. Come and share your master's happiness"* (Matthew 25:21). We can enter into the joy of a more intimate relationship with God as we handle money His way.

2. Money and possessions compete with the Lord for first place in our lives

Money is a primary competitor with Christ for our affection

Money is a primary competitor with Christ for our affection. Jesus tells us we must choose to serve only one of these two masters. *"No one can serve two masters. Either he will hate the one and love the other, or he will be devoted to the one and despise the other. You cannot serve both God and money"* (Matthew 6:24). We use money, but it is impossible for us to serve money and still serve and love God.

During the Crusades of the 12th Century, the Crusaders hired mercenaries to fight for them. Because it was a religious war, the mercenaries were baptised before fighting. Before going under the water, the soldiers would take their swords and hold them up out of the water to symbolise that Jesus Christ was not in control of their weapons. They claimed freedom to use their weapons in any way they wished.

Unfortunately, that illustrates the way many people today handle their money as they hold their wallet or purse 'out of the water.' Their attitude is "God, you may be Lord of my entire life except in the area of money – I am perfectly capable of handling that myself."

3. God wants us to be money-smart

The Lord also talked so much about money because He knew that money problems would be a challenge for all of us. Because He loves and cares for us so deeply, He wanted to equip us to make the wisest possible financial decisions.

A division of responsibilities

Years ago, I embarked on my third and lengthiest topical study of the Bible. I had previously studied subjects such as the biblical account of creation and then I turned to study what the Bible had to say about how we handle our money, wealth and possessions. Along the way I was encouraged by a missionary, Ted Kent, to get out of debt and pay off my mortgage. As I studied the Word I was amazed at how much help and instruction I was able to derive from the Bible on how to handle our finances. I was surprised at how practical the verses were and it was clear to me that a pattern was emerging in the division of responsibilities in the handling of money, wealth and possessions.

Begin the journey

You will discover that learning and applying God's financial principles is a journey that takes time. When we learn God's responsibilities and undertake ours faithfully, we can expect to experience contentment, hope and confidence about our financial future. No matter your circumstances – you may regard yourself as rich or poor – you may be one of those who are in 'fuel poverty' (those whose expenditure on fuel is greater than 10 percent of household income) or unable to make ends meet. You may be in the grips of debt. God has all the answers. Let the journey begin.

> ☐ Please write your prayer requests in your prayer log before coming to the meeting. Please use the first prayer log for yourself on page 148.

[handwritten margin note: If Jesus Christ is not Lord of all, He's not Lord @ all.]

module one
My notes

What I learnt from studying getting started:

The No of verses in the Bible
Bimoney is more than I realise.

What I plan to do differently:

My other notes:

"Everything in the heavens and earth is yours, O Lord"
(1 Chronicles 29:11, TLB)

module two
God's part and our part

The Lord is owner of all

module two
Personal study
To be completed **prior to** module two meeting

Scripture to memorise
"Everything in the heavens and earth is yours, O Lord, and this is your kingdom. We adore you as being in control of everything. Riches and honour come from you alone, and you are the Ruler of all mankind; your hand controls power and might and it is at your discretion that men are made great and given strength" (1 Chronicles 29:11-12, TLB)

Practical application
Continue with your spending tracker and please complete the personal financial statement. Complete the deed of ownership (please bring it to the study to be witnessed by members of your group).

Day one – let's review getting started
Read the getting started notes on pages 4-5 and answer:

1. What information especially interested you?

   2350 – verses in Bible re. finance

2. Comment on any personal challenges you felt after learning the three reasons why the Bible says so much about money.

   to be responsible a steward, of God's things.

God's part and our part

Day two
Read Deuteronomy 10:14; Psalm 24:1 and 1 Corinthians 10:26

1. What do these passages teach about the ownership of your possessions?

   He owns everything & the people.

Read Leviticus 25:23; Psalm 50:10-12 and Haggai 2:8

2. What are some of the specific items that God owns?

   Leviticus 25:23:   God owns land.

   Psalm 50:10-12:   God owns the animals

   Haggai 2:8:   Precious metals.

3. Prayerfully evaluate your attitude of ownership toward your possessions. Do you consistently recognise the true owner of those possessions? Give two practical suggestions to help recognise God's ownership.

   The Bible, ~~reading~~ reading regularly. Language.

Day three
Read Deuteronomy 8:17-18 and 1 Chronicles 29:11-12

1. What do these verses say about your abilities and ownership?   God controls everything, God has given you your abilities,

Read Proverbs 21:1; Isaiah 40:21-24 and Acts 17:26

2. What do these passages tell you about God's ultimate control of people?

   Proverbs 21:1:   God controls the heart.

   Isaiah 40:21-24:   He moves people as He desires.

   Acts 17:26:   He sets time for people.

3. Do you normally recognise the Lord's control? If not, how can you become more consistent in knowing His guiding hand?

He often closes a door, or it goes wrong. Read your Bible + pray every day.

Day four
Read Genesis 45:4-8; Genesis 50:19-20 and Romans 8:28

1. Why is it important to realise that God uses even difficult circumstances for good in the life of a godly person?

God works for the good.

2. How does this perspective impact you today?

Good - Praise God.

3. Share a difficult circumstance you have experienced and how God ultimately used it for good in your life.

Day five
Read Psalm 34:9-10; Matthew 6:31-33 and Philippians 4:19

1. What has the Lord promised concerning meeting your needs?

Put Him first, AND He will meet all your needs.

2. Give an example from the Bible of the Lord providing for someone's needs in a supernatural way.

ISRAEL IN THE WILDERNESS RAVENS FEEDING ELIJAH

3. How do these promises apply to you today?

STILL RELEVANT TODAY

Day six
Read 1 Corinthians 4:2 and Matthew 25:15;19-21

1. According to these verses what are your requirements as a steward?

Faithful Worthyness.
- ness.

2. How would you define a steward?

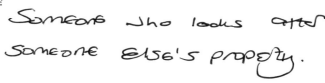

Someone who looks after
someone else's property.

Read Luke 16:1-2

3. Why did the master remove the steward from his position?

Read Luke 16:10

4. Describe the principle found in this verse.

5. How does this apply in your situation?

☐   Please write your prayer requests in your prayer log before coming to the meeting.

module two
Crown notes

To be read after completing **module two** personal study

This is the most important section of the entire study, because how we view God determines how we live. In the Bible God calls Himself by more than 250 names. The name that best describes God's part in the area of money is 'Lord.'

After losing his children and all his possessions, Job continued to worship God because he knew His role as Lord of those possessions. Moses walked away from the treasures of Egypt, choosing instead to suffer with God's people because he accepted God's role as Lord of all. There are three parts to God's position as Lord.

God's part

Ownership

God owns all our possessions. *"To the Lord your God belong…the earth and everything in it"* (Deuteronomy 10:14). *"The earth is the Lord's, and all it contains"* (Psalm 24:1, NASB).

Scripture even reveals specific items God owns. Leviticus 25:23 (KJV) identifies Him as the owner of all the land: *"The land shall not be sold for ever: for the land is mine,"* Haggai 2:8 says that He owns the precious metals: *"'The silver is Mine and the gold is Mine,' declares the Lord Almighty."* And in Psalm 50 we are told that God owns the animals.

"Every animal of the forest is mine, and the cattle on a thousand hills. I know every bird in the mountains, and the creatures of the field are mine. If I were hungry I would not tell you, for the world is mine, and all that is in it."

Psalm 50:10-12

God created all things, and He never transferred the ownership of His creation to people. In Colossians 1:17 (NASB) we are told that *"in Him all things hold together."* At this very moment the Lord holds everything together by His power. As we will see throughout this study, recognising God's ownership is crucial in allowing Jesus Christ to become the Lord of our money and possessions. If christ is not Lord of all, he is not Lord @ all.

Our ownership or his Lordship?

If we are to be genuine followers of Christ, we must transfer ownership of our possessions to Him. *"So therefore, whoever of you does not renounce all that he has cannot be my disciple"* (Luke 14:33, RSV). Sometimes He tests us by asking us to give up the very possessions that are most important to us.

The most vivid example of this in the Bible is when God instructed Abraham *"take now your son, your only son Isaac…and offer him there as a burnt offering"* (Genesis 22:2, NKJV). When

By studying the Bible we can expand our vision of who God is

Abraham obeyed, demonstrating his willingness to give up his most valuable possession, God responded, *"Do not lay your hand on the lad, or do anything to him; for now I know that you fear God, since you have not withheld your son, your only son, from Me"* (Genesis 22:12, NKJV).

When we acknowledge God's ownership, spending decisions become spiritual decisions. No longer do we ask "Lord, what do You want me to do with my money?" It becomes "Lord, what do You want me to do with Your money?" When we have this attitude and handle His money according to His wishes, spending and saving decisions become as spiritual as giving decisions.

God's ownership also influences how we care for possessions, both ours and others. For example, because the Lord is the owner of where we live we want to please Him by keeping His house or apartment clean and in good repair!

Recognising God's ownership

Our culture – the media, even the law – says that what you possess, you own. Acknowledging God's ownership requires a transformation of thinking, and this can be difficult. It is easy to believe intellectually that God owns all you have but still live as if this were not true.

Here are several practical suggestions to help us recognise God's ownership.

- For the next 30 days, meditate on 1 Chronicles 29:11-12 when you first wake and just before going to sleep
- Be careful in the use of personal pronouns; consider substituting 'the' or 'the Lord's 'for 'my,' 'mine,' and 'ours'
- For the next 30 days, ask God to make you aware of His ownership Establish the habit of acknowledging God's ownership every time you purchase an item

Recognising God's ownership is important in learning contentment. When you believe you own a particular possession, circumstances surrounding it will affect your attitude. If it's favourable, you may well feel happy, if it's a difficult circumstance, you will be discontent.

Shortly after Bill Swaim lent me his car, it was written off in an accident. Bill's first reaction was to regret the loss of his car, then he stopped and smiled and said "Lord, it all belongs to you; it never was my car, even though sometimes I felt it was." Bill was learning contentment.

> **God is ultimately in control of every event**

Control

Besides being Creator and Owner, God is ultimately in control of every event. *"We adore you as being in control of everything"* (1 Chronicles 29:11, TLB). *"The Lord does whatever pleases him, in the heavens and on the earth"* (Psalm 135:6). And in the book of Daniel, King Nebuchadnezzar stated: *"I praised the Most High; I honoured and glorified Him who lives forever….He does as He pleases with the powers of heaven and the peoples of the earth. No one can hold back His hand or say to him: 'What have you done?'"* (Daniel 4:34-35).

God is also able to exert His control in difficult circumstances. *"I am the Lord, and there is none else. I form the light, and create darkness: I make peace, and create evil: I the Lord do all these things"* (Isaiah 45:6-7, KJV).

It is important for us to realise that our heavenly Father uses even seemingly devastating circumstances for ultimate good in the lives of the godly. *"We know that in all things God works for the good of those who love him, who have been called according to his purpose"* (Romans 8:28). The Lord allows difficult circumstances for three reasons:

1. He accomplishes his intentions

This is illustrated in the life of Joseph, who was sold into slavery as a teenager by his jealous brothers. Joseph later said to his brothers: *"do not be distressed and do not be angry with yourselves for selling me here, because it was to save lives that God sent me ahead of you.... It was not you who sent me here, but God.... You intended to harm me, but God intended it for good"* (Genesis 45:5, 8; 50:20).

2. He develops our character

Godly character, something that is precious in the sight of God, is often developed during trying times. *"We rejoice in our sufferings, knowing that suffering produces endurance, and endurance produces character"* (Romans 5:3-4, RSV).

3. He disciplines His children

"Those whom the Lord loves He disciplines.... He disciplines us for our good, so that we may share His holiness. All discipline for the moment seems not to be joyful, but sorrowful; yet to those who have been trained by it, afterwards it yields the peaceful fruit of righteousness."
Hebrews 12:6, 10-11, NASB WHEN YOURE DOWN TO NOTHING GOD'S UP TO SOMETHING.

When we are disobedient, we can expect our loving Lord to discipline us, often through difficult circumstances. His purpose is to encourage us to abandon our sin and "share His holiness." You can be at peace knowing that your loving heavenly Father is in control of every situation you will ever face. He will use every one of them for a good purpose.

Regardless of how He chooses to provide for our needs, God is completely reliable

God is the provider

The Lord promises to provide our needs. *"Seek first His kingdom and His righteousness, and all these things (food, shelter and clothing) shall be given to you"* (Matthew 6:33).

The same Lord who fed manna to the children of Israel during their 40 years of wandering in the wilderness and who fed more than 5,000 with only five loaves and two fish has promised to provide our needs. This is the same Lord who told Elijah *"I have commanded the ravens to provide for you.... The ravens brought him bread and meat in the morning and bread and meat in the evening"* (1 Kings 17:4 , 6, NASB).

God is both predictable and unpredictable. God is totally predictable in His faithfulness to provide for our needs. What we cannot predict is how He will provide. He uses different and often surprising means — an increase in income, a reduction in cost, a state allowance/benefit or a gift. He may provide an opportunity to stretch limited resources through sales or discounts. Regardless of how He chooses to provide for our needs, God is completely reliable.

History records a story that illustrates this principle. As World War II was drawing to a close, the Allied armies gathered up many orphans and placed them in camps where they were well fed. But despite excellent care, the orphans were afraid and slept poorly.

Finally, a doctor came up with a solution. When the children were put to bed, he gave each of them a piece of bread to hold. Any hungry children could get more to eat, but when they were finished, they would still have this piece of bread just to hold — not to eat.

This piece of bread produced wonderful results. The children went to bed knowing instinctively they would have food to eat the next day. That guarantee gave them restful sleep.

Similarly, God has given us His guarantee — our 'piece of bread.' As we cling to His promises of provision, we can relax and be content. *"My God shall supply all your needs according to His glorious riches…"* (Philippians 4:19).

Needs versus wants

The Lord instructs us to be content when our basic needs are met. *"If we have food and clothing, we will be content"* (1 Timothy 6:8). It is important to understand the difference between a need and a want. Needs are the basic necessities of life — food, clothing, and shelter. Wants are anything in excess of needs. God may allow us to have our wants, but He has not promised to provide all of them.

Getting to know God

God, as He is revealed in Scripture, is very different from most people imagine. We tend to shrink Him down to our human abilities and limitations, forgetting that He *"stretched out the heavens and laid the foundations of the earth"* (Isaiah 51:13). By studying the Bible we can expand our vision of who He is. The following are a just a few samples.

He is Lord of the universe

Carefully review some of His names and attributes: Creator, the Almighty, eternal, all-knowing, all-powerful, awesome, Lord of Lords and King of kings. God's power and ability are beyond our understanding.

Astronomers estimate that there are more than 100 billion galaxies in the universe, each containing billions of stars. The distance from one end of a galaxy to the other is often measured in millions of light years. Though our sun is a relatively small star, it could contain more than one million earths, and it has temperatures of 20 million degrees at its centre. Isaiah wrote, *"Lift up your eyes on high and see who has created these stars…. He calls them all by name; because of the greatness of His might and the strength of His power, not one of them is missing"* (Isaiah 40:26, NASB).

He is Lord of the nations

God established the nations. Acts 17:26 says, *"He (the Lord)…scattered the nations across the face of the earth. He decided beforehand which should rise and fall, and when. He determined their boundaries"* (TLB).

God is far above all national leaders and powers. Isaiah 40:21-23 (NASB) tells us *"do you not know? Have you not heard?…It is He who sits above the circle of the earth, and its inhabitants are like grasshoppers….He it is who reduces rulers to nothing, who makes the judges of the earth meaningless."* From Isaiah 40:15, 17 (NASB) we read *"the nations are like a drop from a bucket, and are regarded as a speck of dust on the scales….All the nations are as nothing before Him."*

Your questions

Q: I'm totally frustrated! God says He's going to provide my needs. So, what's there for me to do? Do I have to go to work?

A: God has certain responsibilities when it comes to money, and He's given others to us. He's promised to provide our needs, and at the same time He wants us to work hard — for many reasons. He usually provides our needs through our work.

God is very different than most people imagine

15

He is Lord of the individual

Psalm 139:3-4, 16 reveals God's involvement with each of us as individuals. *"You discern my going out and my lying down; you are familiar with all my ways. Before a word is on my tongue you know it completely, O Lord…all the days ordained for me were written in your book before one of them came to be."* The Lord is so involved in our lives that He reassures us *"the very hairs of your head are all numbered"* (Matthew 10:30, KJV). Our heavenly Father is the One who knows us the best and loves us the most.

God hung the stars in space, fashioned the earth's towering mountains and mighty oceans, and determined the destiny of nations. Jeremiah observed: *"there is nothing too hard for You"* (Jeremiah 32:17, NKJV). Yet God knows when a sparrow falls to the ground. Nothing in this study is more important than catching the vision of who God is and what responsibilities He retains in our finances.

Summary of God's part

The Lord did not design people to shoulder the responsibilities that only He can carry. Jesus said *"come to me, all you who are weary and burdened, and I will give you rest. Take my yoke upon you and learn from me, for I am gentle and humble in heart, and you will find rest for your souls. For my yoke is easy and my burden is light"* (Matthew 11:28-30). God has assumed the burdens of ownership, control, and provision. For this reason, His yoke is easy and we can rest and enjoy the peace of God.

For most of us, the primary problem is failing to consistently recognise God's part. Our culture believes that God plays no part in financial matters, and we have, in some measure, been influenced by that view.

Another reason for this difficulty is that God has chosen to be invisible. Anything that is "out of sight" tends to become "out of mind." We get out of the habit of recognising His ownership, control and provision.

After learning God's part, you might wonder whether He's left any responsibilities for us. The Lord has given us great responsibility.

Our part

A steward is a manager of someone else's possessions

The word that best describes our part is *steward*. A steward is a manager of someone else's possessions. God has given us the authority to be stewards. *"You made him ruler over the works of your (the Lord's) hands; you put everything under his feet"* (Psalm 8:6).

Our responsibility is summed up in this verse: *"It is required of stewards that one be found faithful"* (1 Corinthians 4:2, NASB). Before we can be faithful, we must know what we are required to do. Just as the purchaser of new technology studies the manufacturer's manual to learn how to operate it, we need to examine our manufacturer's handbook — the Bible — to determine how He wants us to handle His possessions.

As we begin to study our responsibilities, it's important to remember that God loves and cares for us deeply. He is a God of mercy and grace. He has given us these principles because He wants the best for us. Most people discover areas in which they have not been faithful. Don't become discouraged. Simply seek to apply faithfully what you learn.

Now, let's examine two important elements of our responsibility.

1. Be faithful with what we are given

We are to be faithful regardless of how much God entrusts to us. The parable of the talents (a talent was a sum of money) illustrates this. *"For the kingdom of heaven is like a man travelling to a far country, who called his own servants and delivered his goods to them. To one he gave five talents, to another two, and to another one"* (Matthew 25:14-15, NKJV).

When the owner returned, he held each one responsible for faithfully managing his possessions. The owner praised the faithful servant who received five talents: *"Well done, good and faithful servant; you were faithful over a few things, I will make you ruler over many things. Enter into the joy of your Lord"* (Matthew 25:21, NKJV). Interestingly, the servant who had been given two talents received the identical reward as the one who had been given five (see Matthew 25:23). God rewards faithfulness regardless of the amount over which we are responsible.

We are required to be faithful whether we are given much or little. As someone once said, "It's not what I would do if £1 million were my lot; it's what I am doing with the £10 I've got."

2. Be faithful in every area

God wants us to be faithful in handling all of our money. Unfortunately, most Christians have been taught how to handle only 10 percent of their income God's way – the area of giving. And although this area is crucial, so is the other 90 percent, which is frequently handled from the world's perspective.

As a result of not being taught to handle money biblically, many Christians have wrong attitudes toward possessions. This often causes them to make poor financial decisions with painful consequences. Hosea 4:6 reads, *"my people are destroyed from lack of knowledge."*

Benefits of handling money faithfully

The faithful steward enjoys three benefits.

1. More intimate fellowship with Jesus Christ

Remember what the master said to the servant who had been faithful with his finances: *"come and share your master's happiness"* (Matthew 25:21). We can enter into closer fellowship with our Lord when we are faithful with the possessions He has given us.

Someone once said that God often allows a person to teach a subject because the teacher needs it! That is true for many in the area of money. While my life started in relative poverty I subsequently enjoyed more wealth than some and found how easy it was to trust in being financially comfortable. If you allow God's Word to mould your attitude you will find, a dramatic improvement in your fellowship with the Lord. You will gain a deeper understanding of His purpose for your life when you yield your will to His in this area of your life in Him – exactly what He intends.

2. The development of character

God uses money to refine character. As David McConaughy explained in his book, *Money the Acid Test* (written in 1918), "Money, most common of temporal things, involves uncommon and eternal consequences. Even though it may be done quite unconsciously, money moulds people in the process of getting it, saving it, spending it, and giving it. Depending on how it's used, it proves to be a blessing or a curse. Either the person becomes master of the money, or the money becomes the master of the person. Our Lord uses money to test our lives and as an instrument to mould us into the likeness of Himself."

All through Scripture there is a correlation between the development of people's character and how they handle money. Money is regarded as an index to a person's true character. You have heard the expression 'money talks,' and indeed it does. You can tell a lot about a person's character by examining his or her cheque book and credit card statement because we spend our money on the things that are most important to us.

3. Having our finances in order

As we apply God's principles to our finances, we will begin to get out of debt, spend more wisely, start saving for our future, and give even more to the work of Christ.

Principles of faithfulness

We can draw important principles of faithfulness from the Lord's parables:

1. If we waste possessions, God may remove us as stewards

"There was a rich man whose manager (steward) was accused of wasting his possessions. So he called him in and asked him, 'What is this I hear about you? Give an account of your management, because you cannot be manager (steward) any longer.'"
Luke 16:1-2

If you waste the possessions entrusted to you, you may not be given more

Two principles from this passage are applicable to us. First, when we waste our possessions it becomes public knowledge and creates a poor testimony. *"(The manager) was accused of wasting his possessions."* Second, God may remove us as stewards if we squander what He has given to us.

A businessman earned a fortune in just three years and then went on a spending spree. Two years later he informed his office staff that he had little left and everyone would need to economise. Shortly thereafter, he left for an expensive holiday and had his office completely renovated at a cost of thousands of pounds. God soon removed this man from the privilege of being steward over much, and eventually he found himself almost bankrupt.

If you waste the possessions entrusted to you, you may not be given more.

2. We must be faithful in little things

"Whoever can be trusted with very little can also be trusted with much, and whoever is dishonest with very little will also be dishonest with much."
Luke 16:10

How do you know if your son is going to take good care of his first car? Observe how he cared for his bicycle. How do you know if a salesperson will do a competent job of serving a large customer? Evaluate how they serve a small customer. If we have the character to be faithful with small things, God knows He can trust us with greater responsibilities. Small things are small things, but faithfulness with a small thing is a big thing.

3. We must be faithful with another's possessions

Faithfulness with another's possessions in some measure will determine how much you are given. *"And if you have not been trustworthy with someone else's property, who will give you property of your own?"* (Luke 16:12).

This is a principle that is often overlooked. One of Howard Dayton's friends rented a vehicle from a friend and damaged it in an accident, he told the owner what happened and then delivered the vehicle to the owner's mechanic with these instructions: "make it better than it was before the accident, and I will be responsible for the bill." What an example!

When someone allows you to use something, are you careful to return it promptly and in good shape? Are you careless with your employer's office or plant supplies? Do you waste electricity when you are staying in a hotel room? Some people have not been entrusted with more because they have been unfaithful with the possessions of others.

God promises to do His part in our finances; our part is to grow in faithfulness.

module two
My notes

What I learnt from studying God's part and our part:

What I plan to do differently:

My other notes:

> **"Whatever you do, do your work heartily, as for the Lord rather than for men....It is the Lord Christ whom you serve"**
> **(Colossians 3:23-24, NASB)**

module three
Work

Work diligently as unto the Lord

module three
Personal study

To be completed **prior to** module three meeting

Scripture to memorise
"Whatever you do, do your work heartily, as for the Lord rather than for men....It is the Lord Christ whom you serve" (Colossians 3:23-24, NASB)

Practical application
Please continue to complete your spending tracker. Read the spending budget hints and complete your Idea List.

Day one – let's review God's part/our part
Read the God's part/our part notes on pages 12-19 and answer:

1. How have you observed God using money to mould your character?

2. What strengths have been developed in your character?

3. What weaknesses in your character still need to be addressed?

Work

Day two
Read Genesis 2:15

1. Why is it important to recognise that the Lord created work before sin entered the world?

Read Genesis 3:17-19

2. What was the consequence of sin on work?

Read Exodus 20:9 and 2 Thessalonians 3:10-12

3. What do these passages say to you about work?

Exodus 20:9:

2 Thessalonians 3:10-12:

Day three
Read Genesis 39:2-5; Exodus 35:30-35; Exodus 36:1-2; Psalm 75:6-7 and Proverbs 22:29

1. What do these verses tell us about the Lord's involvement in our work?

Genesis 39:2-5:

Exodus 35:30-35:

Exodus 36:1-2:

Psalm 75:6-7:

Proverbs 22:29:

2. How do these truths differ from the way most people view work?

3. How will the truths you have discovered impact your work?

Day four
Read Ephesians 6:5-9; Leviticus 19:13b and Colossians 3:22-4:1

1. What responsibilities do the employee and employer have according to these verses?

    Employee responsibilities:

    Employer responsibilities:

2. For whom do you really work? How will this understanding change your work performance?

Day five
Read Proverbs 6:6-11; Proverbs 18:9 and 2 Thessalonians 3:7-9

1. What does God say about working hard?

    Proverbs 6:6-11:

    Proverbs 18:9:

    2 Thessalonians 3:7-9:

2. Do you work hard? If not, what can you do to improve your work practices?

Read Exodus 34:21

3. What does this verse communicate to you about rest?

4. Do you get enough rest?

5. How do you guard against working too much?

6. Do you need to make changes in your work/life balance?

Day six
Read Proverbs 31:10-28; Titus 2:4-5 and Acts 16:14-16

1. What do these passages tell us about women working?

   Proverbs 31:10-28:

   Titus 2:4-5:

   Acts 16:14-16:

2. If you are a woman, how does this apply to your situation?

Read 2 Corinthians 6:14-18

3. How does this concept of 'yoking' or 'being bound together' apply to partnerships in business and work?

4. Can you give any examples from the Bible of people who retired?

5. Do you think retirement, as it is practiced in our culture, is biblically acceptable? Why or why not?

☐ **Please write your prayer requests in your prayer log before coming to the meeting.**

module three
Crown notes

To be read after completing **module three** personal study

Over a lifetime, the average person spends 60,000 to 70,000 hours working. But, often with the job comes some degree of dissatisfaction. Perhaps no statistic demonstrates this more than job-change frequency. A survey found that the one in three workers remain in a job for less than two years while 20 percent of those polled were thinking of changing their job in the next year. Money was cited as the main reason for the change.

Boredom, lack of fulfillment, inadequate income, rising food and household costs, high energy costs and countless other pressures have contributed to this discontentment. Blue collar workers, office and shop staff, sales people, managers, all — regardless of profession — have expressed similar frustrations. Understanding scriptural principles that relate to work will help you find satisfaction in your job. Implementing them will position you to increase your income.

God's perspective of work

One of the primary purposes of work is to develop character

Despite what many believe, work was initiated for our benefit in the sinless environment of the garden of Eden. Work is not a result of the curse! *"The Lord God placed the man in the Garden of Eden to tend and watch over it"* (Genesis 2:15, NLT). The very first thing God did with Adam was to put him to work.

After the fall, work became more difficult. *"Cursed is the ground because of you; through painful toil you will eat of it all the days of your life. It will produce thorns and thistles for you, and you will eat the plants of the field. By the sweat of your brow you will eat your food"* (Genesis 3:17-19).

Work is so important that in Exodus 34:21 God gives this command: *"six days you shall labour."* The Apostle Paul is just as direct: *"if a man will not work, he shall not eat"* (2 Thessalonians 3:10). Examine the verse carefully. It says *"if a man will not work."* It does not say, "If anyone cannot work." This principle does not apply to those who are physically or mentally unable to work; it is for those who are able but choose not to work.

A close friend has a sister in her mid-40s whose parents have always supported her. She has never had to face the responsibilities and hardships involved in a job. Consequently, her character has not been properly developed, leaving her hopelessly immature in many areas of his life.

One of the primary purposes of work is to develop character. While the carpenter is building a house, the house is also building the carpenter. The carpenter's skill, diligence, manual dexterity, and judgement are refined. A job is not merely a task designed to earn money; it's also intended to produce godly character in the life of the worker.

All honest trades and professions are honourable

Scripture gives dignity to all types of work, not elevating any honest trade or profession above another. David was a shepherd and a king. Luke was a doctor. Lydia was a retailer of purple fabric. Daniel was a government worker. Paul was a tent maker. Mary was a homemaker. And, finally, the Lord Jesus was a carpenter.

In God's economy, there is equal dignity in the labour of the car mechanic and the CEO of a bank, in the labour of the pastor and an administrator serving the church.

God's part in work

Scripture reveals three responsibilities the Lord has in our work.

1. God gives job skills

Exodus 36:1 (NASB) illustrates this truth: *"Every skillful person in whom the Lord has put skill and understanding to know how to perform all the work…shall perform."* God has given each of us unique aptitudes. People have a wide variety of abilities, manual skills, and intellectual capacities. It is not a matter of one person being better than another, merely that each has received different abilities.

2. God ultimately gives success

The life of Joseph is a perfect example of God helping a person to succeed. *"The Lord was with Joseph and he prospered, and he lived in the house of his Egyptian master. When his master saw that the Lord was with him and that the Lord gave him success in everything he did"* (Genesis 39:2-3). Although we have certain responsibilities, it is ultimately God who gives success.

3. God directs our paths

In Proverbs 3: 5-6 we learn that if we put God first and *"trust in the Lord with all your heart and lean not on your own understanding. In all your ways acknowledge Him and He will make your paths straight."* One author wrote a book called 'Thank God it's Monday' which is all about bringing God into the workplace. Ultimately matters such as career development, promotion, remuneration are not just about us and our desires but about seeking God's path for our work. Many people leave God out of their work, believing that they alone are responsible for their abilities and successes. One of the major reasons they experience stress and frustration in their jobs is because they don't understand God's part in their work. Consider for a few minutes; If God gives you your abilities and has a purpose for your life including every aspect of your working life, how should this perspective affect your work?

Recognising that we work for the Lord has profound implications

Our part in work

Did you know that in our work we actually serve God rather than men? *"Whatever you do, do your work heartily, as for the Lord rather than for men….It is the Lord Christ whom you serve"* (Colossians 3:23-24, NASB). Recognising that we work for God has profound implications.

If you could see Jesus Christ as your boss, would you try to be more faithful in your job? The most important question you need to answer every day as you begin your work is this: "for whom do I work?" You work for Christ.

Work hard

"Whatever your hand finds to do, do it with all your might" (Ecclesiastes 9:10). *"The precious possession of a man is diligence"* (Proverbs 12:27, NASB). Scripture encourages hard work and diligence; laziness is condemned: *"one who is slack in his work is brother to one who destroys"* (Proverbs 18:9).

Paul's life was an example of hard work. *"We worked night and day, labouring and toiling so that we would not be a burden to any of you…in order to make ourselves a model for you to follow"* (2 Thessalonians 3:8-9).

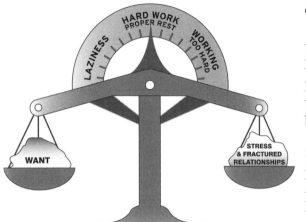

A balanced life with contentment

Your work should never be at such a level that people will equate laziness or poor timekeeping with God. Nothing less than hard work and the pursuit of excellence pleases Him. He does not require us to be 'super workers' who never make mistakes, but He does expect us to do the best we possibly can.

But do not overwork!

Hard work, however, must be balanced by the other priorities of life. If your job demands so much of your time and energy that you neglect your relationship with Christ or your loved ones, then you are working too much. Determine whether the job itself is too demanding or whether your work habits need changing. If you tend to be a workaholic, be careful not to shortchange the other priorities of life.

Exodus 34:21 reads *"six days you shall labour, but on the seventh day you shall rest; even during the ploughing season and harvest you must rest."* We believe this Old Testament principle of resting one day out of seven has application today. This has been difficult for me, particularly during times of 'ploughing or harvesting,' when a project deadline approaches or I am under financial pressure.

Rest can become an issue of faith. Is God able to make our six days of work more productive than seven? Yes! The Lord instituted weekly rest for our physical, mental, and spiritual health. Study this illustration to understand the balance God wants in our lives.

Employer responsibilities

Godly employers perform a balancing act. They are to love, serve, and encourage employees while leading them and holding them accountable for the completion of their assigned tasks. Let's examine several principles that should govern an employer's conduct.

1. Serve your employees

The basis for biblical leadership is servanthood: *"whoever wants to become great among you must be your servant"* (Matthew 20:26). Employers often concentrate on producing a profit at the expense of their personnel. However, the Bible directs them to balance efforts to make a profit with an unselfish concern for employees, treating them with fairness and dignity. *"Masters (employers), provide your slaves (employees) with what is right and fair, because you know that you also have a Master in heaven"* (Colossians 4:1).

Employers should attempt to be creative as they serve their employees. For example, investing time and money to educate and upgrade their employees' job skills will help employees grow in value and earning power.

2. Be a good communicator

The Genesis account of building the tower of Babel supports the importance of good communication. At that time, everyone spoke the same language and adopted a common goal. The Lord makes this remarkable observation *"if as one people speaking the same language they have begun to do this, then nothing they plan to do will be impossible for them"* (Genesis 11:6).

When people have good communication and pursue a common goal, then "nothing they plan to do will be impossible for them" – as long as it's within the will of God. Since building the tower was not what He wanted, He stopped construction. And how did God do it? He disrupted their ability to communicate, which was the foundation for successfully completing the tower. *"Come, let us go down and confuse their language so they will not understand each other"* (Genesis 11:7).

It is especially important to listen to employee complaints. *"If I have despised the claim of my…(employees) when they filed a complaint against me, what then could I do when God arises? And when He calls me to account, what will I answer Him?"* (Job 31:13-15, NASB). A sensitive, listening ear is a tangible expression of care. When a complaint is legitimate, employers should take appropriate steps to solve the problem.

3. Hold employees accountable

Employers are responsible for employees knowing what is expected on the job. Employers should regularly evaluate employee performance and communicate it to them. Employees who do not perform satisfactorily and are unable or unwilling to change may, for example, require additional training.

4. Pay your employees a fair wage promptly

The Bible warns employers to pay a fair wage. *"(The Lord will judge) those who defraud labourers of their wages"* (Malachi 3:5). It also commands them to pay wages promptly when due. *"Do not take advantage of a hired man…pay him his wages each day before sunset…otherwise he may cry to the Lord against you, and you will be guilty of sin"* (Deuteronomy 24:14-15).

5. Pray for godly employees

God may choose to bless an employer for having a godly employee. Scripture gives two examples of this. First, *"Laban said to (Jacob), 'If I have found favour in your eyes, please stay;…the Lord has blessed me because of you'"* (Genesis 30:27). Second, *"Joseph found favour in (Potiphar's) eyes…from the time he put him in charge of his household and of all that he owned, the Lord blessed the household of the Egyptian because of Joseph. The blessing of the Lord was on everything Potiphar had, both in the house and in the field"* (Genesis 39:4-5).

Your questions

Q: I've been using a spending plan and don't spend one penny on anything that is not an absolute need, but I'm still not able to make ends meet. What should I do?

A: You're simply not earning enough money. You need to find a job for which you are well-suited that will produce more income. I'd start by taking an aptitude test to identify your best potential careers. Then pray and ask the Lord the action and direction you should take.

This principle was my primary reason for employing Dave, an especially godly accountant. He was technically very capable, always up-to-date and had a mind for detail that was essential in the cut and thrust of a professional business. He worked in an office with 15 other staff and his influence was tangible. There was less profanity, he was an excellent model of hard work and was liked by all the staff for his ability to motivate and train. This principle is not a command, but we believe it is wise to bring 'Daves' into a business.

Employee responsibilities

We can identify six major responsibilities of godly employees by examining the story of Daniel in the lion's den. In the sixth chapter of Daniel, Darius, the king of Babylon, appointed 120 people to administer the government, and three people – one of whom was Daniel – to supervise the administrators. Because of Daniel's outstanding service, King Darius decided to promote Daniel to govern the entire kingdom. Daniel's jealous peers looked for a way to disqualify him but could find no basis for accusation. Knowing Daniel's devotion to God, they asked King Darius to enact a law requiring everyone to worship only the king or die in the lion's den. Daniel refused to stop worshipping God, and Darius reluctantly threw him to the lions. When God rescued Daniel by sending an angel to shut the lions' mouths, the thankful king ordered all of his subjects to honour the God of Daniel. Daniel modeled the six characteristics of godly employees.

1. Honesty

Daniel 6:4 tells us that Daniel's fellow employees could find no dishonesty in him, and there was no 'evidence of corruption' in his work. Daniel was an example of total honesty, the crucial character quality we will study in the module on honesty.

2. Faithfulness

We discover the second characteristic of godly employees in Daniel 6:4 (KJV): *"He was faithful."* godly employees strive for the goal of being faithful and excellent in work.

3. Prayerfulness

Godly employees are people of prayer. *"When Daniel learned that the decree had been published (restricting worship to the king alone)…he went home to his upstairs room where the windows opened towards Jerusalem. Three times a day he got down on his knees and prayed, giving thanks to his God, just as he had done before"* (Daniel 6:10). Daniel shouldered the responsibility of governing the most powerful country of his day. Few of us will ever face that kind of pressure or demands on our time. Yet he knew the importance of prayer. If you are not praying consistently, your work is suffering.

4. Loyalty – honours the employer

"Daniel answered, 'O king, live for ever!'" (Daniel 6:21). What a remarkable response from Daniel. The king had been tricked into sentencing Daniel to the lion's den. But Daniel's reaction was to honour his employer. Think how easy it would have been to disrespect the king and say something like "you fool! The God who sent His angel to shut the lions' mouths is now going to knock you out!" Instead, he honoured his employer.

Godly employees always honour their superiors. *"Slaves (employees), submit yourselves to your masters (employers) with all respect, not only to those who are good and considerate, but also to those who are harsh"* (1 Peter 2:18). One way we honour employers is refusing to gossip, or bad mouth them behind their backs regardless of their shortcomings.

5. Honours fellow employees

People may damage your reputation or may even attempt to have you sacked or transferred from your job to secure a promotion over you. Not only did they do that to Daniel, they even tried to murder him. Despite this, there is no evidence that he did anything but honour his fellow employees. *"Do not slander a servant (employee) to his master (employer), or he will curse you"* (Proverbs 30:10).

Godly employees avoid workplace politics and manipulation to secure a promotion. Your boss does not control your promotion; God does. You can be content in your job as you focus on being faithful, honouring superiors, and encouraging other employees. Having done this you can rest, knowing that Christ will promote you if and when He chooses.

6. Verbalises faith

King Darius would never have known about God if Daniel had not communicated his faith at appropriate moments while at work. *"When he (the king) came near the den, he called to Daniel in an anguished voice, Daniel, servant of the living God, has your God, whom you serve continually, been able to rescue you from the lions?'"* (Daniel 6:20). Daniel's words and actions influenced King Darius, who observed his honesty, faithfulness, and hard work. Listen to the king's response: *"I issue a decree that in every part of my kingdom people must fear and reverence the God of Daniel. For he is the living God and he endures for ever"* (Daniel 6:26).

Daniel influenced his employer, one of the most powerful people in the world, to believe in the only true God. You have that same opportunity in your God-given sphere of work. Let us say this another way. A job well done earns you the right to tell those you work with about salvation and the reality of Christ. Viewing your work from God's perspective turns dissatisfaction to contentment with a job well done; drudgery becomes excitement over the prospect of introducing others to the Saviour.

Other work issues

Ambition

Scripture does not condemn ambition. Paul was ambitious. *"We make it our goal to please him"* (2 Corinthians 5:9). The Bible does, however, condemn selfish ambition. The Lord *"will give to each person according to what he has done…for those who are self-seeking…wrath and anger"* (Romans 2:6, 8, NASB). *"But if you have…selfish ambition in your heart, do not be arrogant and so lie against the truth. This wisdom is not that which comes down from above, but is earthly, natural, demonic. For where…selfish ambition exist, there is disorder and every evil thing"* (James 3:14-16). *"Should you then seek great things for yourself? Seek them not"* (Jeremiah 45:5).

Remember, the Bible is not the enemy of ambition, only of the wrong type of ambition. Our ambition should be to please Christ, work hard and pursue excellence in our job to please Him.

Your calling

God has given each of us a specific calling or purpose. *"We are God's workmanship, created in Christ Jesus to do good works, which God prepared in advance for us to do"* (Ephesians 2:10). Study this passage carefully. *"We are His workmanship."* The *Amplified® Bible* says, *"We are His handiwork."* God has given each of us special physical, emotional, and mental abilities. You may have heard the expression "after the Lord made you, He threw away the mould." It's true! You are gifted uniquely. No one in all of history — past, present or future — is like you.

The passage continues *"created in Christ Jesus for good works, which God prepared beforehand so that we would walk in them."* God created each of us for a particular task, endowing us with the abilities and desires to accomplish it. Your calling may be full-time Christian service or a secular job.

People often wonder whether God wants them to continue in their work after they commit their lives to Christ. Many feel they are not serving Him in a significant way if they remain at their jobs. Nothing could be further from the truth. The key is for each person to identify God's call for his or her life. While in business I endeavoured to be at the leading edge in practicing good management principles. Although I believe in the application of good business principles, I place far more confidence in the belief that I have a call from God. While I was working in business, I knew it was a calling to business, but all the time God was preparing us for the work with Crown. Wherever we are, whatever we do, He wants us to be of service to Him. Having been involved in prison ministry I have seen how God uses those who love Him and are inside detention centres. Make yourself available to Him — your pulpit is where you are.

To those who earn a living through secular pursuits, it is a great comfort to know that the 'call' of holy vocation carries over into all walks of life. The key is for us to identify God's call for our lives, recognising that God strategically places His children everywhere!

Partnerships

God strategically places his children everywhere!

Scripture discourages business partnerships with those who do not know Christ. In 2 Corinthians 6:14-17 (NLT) we read *"don't team up with those who are unbelievers. How can righteousness be a partner with wickedness? How can light live with darkness?…How can a believer be a partner with an unbeliever?…Therefore, come out from among believers, and separate yourselves from them, says the Lord."* Many have suffered financially for violating this principle.

In our opinion, we should be careful about entering into any partnership, even with another Christian. With my lifetime of contacts, I would consider only a few people as partners. These are people I know well. I have observed their commitment to the Lord. I know their strengths and weaknesses and have seen them handle money faithfully.

If, after prayerful consideration, you decide to form a partnership, first take the time to commit your understandings into writing. Develop this agreement with your future partner, and be sure to include a way to end the partnership. If you are not able to agree in writing, do not become partners. Remember, do not rush into a partnership!

Procrastination

A procrastinator is someone who, because of laziness or fear, has a habit of putting things off until later. This habit often develops into a serious character flaw.

The book of Ruth introduces Boaz, one of my favorite examples in the Bible of a non-procrastinator. Ruth's mother-in-law, Naomi, made this revealing comment about Ruth's future husband, Boaz: *"sit still, my daughter, until you know how the matter will turn out; for the man will not rest until he has concluded the matter this day"* (Ruth 3:18, NKJV). Boaz had a reputation for acting promptly.

Here are some practical suggestions to help overcome procrastination:

1. List the things you need to do each day
2. Prayerfully review the list and prioritise it according to the tasks you need to accomplish first
3. Finish the first task on your list before starting the second. Often that first task is the most difficult or the one you fear the most
4. Ask God to give you courage, remembering Philippians 4:13 (NKJV) *"I can do all things through Christ who strengthens me."*

Wives working outside the home

For many reasons, women work in jobs of all kinds. Married women generally work to provide additional income for their families, to express their creativity, or because they enjoy their jobs.

In our opinion, unless family finances prohibit it, it is wise during the children's early formative years for the mother (or maybe the father) to be home while the children are home. Titus 2:4-5 reads *"train the younger women to love their husbands and children, to be self-controlled and pure, to be busy at home."* As the children mature, a mother will have increased freedom to pursue outside work.

Proverbs 31:10-27 (NASB) reads *"an excellent wife…does him (her husband) good and not evil all the days of her life. She looks for wool and flax and works with her hands….She brings her food from afar. She rises also while it is still night and gives food to her household….She considers a field and buys it; from her earnings she plants a vineyard….She stretches out her hands to the distaff, and her hands grasp the spindle. She extends her hand to the poor….She makes coverings for herself; her clothing is fine linen and purple. Her husband is known in the gates, when he sits among the elders of the land. She makes linen garments and sells them, and supplies belts to the tradesmen….She looks well to the ways of her household, and does not eat the bread of idleness."*

Proverbs 31 paints a picture of the working wife living a balanced life with the thrust of her activity toward the home. Some women are gifted as homemakers; there is no more important task than raising godly children. Others may have skills they desire to express in work outside the home, and some must work to earn income. A survey revealed that today only a third of parents think having a job helps set a positive role model for their children. Eighty percent of mums reported in a survey that they considered the main benefit of being in work as having more money to pay bills and do things as a family.

Either way, it is a decision that the married couple should make together.

Did you know?

Many have widespread dissatisfaction with their jobs. One in three remain in a job for less than two years.

Two income families

If both the husband and wife work outside the home, it is worth examining how much income, after taxes and expenses, the second income contributes. The "Example 1" column of the worksheet below makes the following assumptions: 35 hours a week at £7 per hour; giving 10 percent of the gross income; tax and national insurance; ten trips per week of five miles at a cost of 30 pence a mile; lunch, snacks, and coffee breaks of £13 per week; eating out more often and using convenience foods add £10 a week to the spending plan; £5 for extra clothing and cleaning; £5 more for grooming; extra child care of £120 a week. The 'Example 2' column assumes earning £15 an hour; all other assumptions remain the same.

These assumptions are for illustration only and may not represent your situation. Complete the exercise below to determine your actual income after expenses.

Income and spending for second wage earner	Example 1	Example 2	My situation
Gross yearly income	£12,740	£27,300	
Gross weekly income	£245	£525	
Add: CTC and WTC	£44	£52	
	£289	£577	
Expenses:			
Giving	29	58	
Income tax*	22	77	
National insurance*	15	46	
Transportation	15	15	
Lunch/snacks/breaks	13	13	
Restaurants/convenience food	10	10	
Extra clothing/cleaning	5	5	
Personal grooming	5	5	
Child care	120	120	
Total expenses	£234	£349	
Net additional income per week	£55	£228	
Net income per hour	£1.57	£6.51	

*This approximate liability does not take into account childcare vouchers. Where childcare vouchers are available from your employer there will be a saving which will significantly reduce the tax and national insurance liability. This could amount to more than 50p an hour depending on your circumstances.

Considering what to do

Couples are often surprised to learn that the income earned by a second working spouse is not as much as they had expected. Some have actually produced more net income (after reducing work-related expenses) when they decided to work in some creative way while staying at home. Of course, the financial benefits are not the only factors to evaluate. Also consider the physical and emotional demands of working and how they affect a family.

Tax credits make a difference

Child Tax Credit (CTC) can generally be claimed by families with at least one child, subject to certain income criteria. It provides support for children until 1 September after their 16th birthday and, in certain circumstances, for children aged 16 to 18. The amount of benefit is dependent on the number of children in the family, whether they have disabilities and the total family income. It will be paid direct to the person who cares for the children.

CTC is made up of the following elements:

1. A family element that is payable to any family responsible for a child. It is paid at a higher rate to families with at least one child under the age of one.
2. A child element for each child the family is responsible for. This is paid at a higher rate if the child has a disability and at an enhanced rate for a child with a severe disability.
3. Working Tax Credit (WTC) is a tax credit for people in paid work who are on a relatively low income (for couples, joint income), including those with a disability. It also includes support for the cost of eligible childcare.

WTC is for people who are employed or self-employed (either on their own or in partnership) who:

- usually work 16 hours or more a week
- are paid for that work, and
- expect to work for at least 4 weeks

and who are:

- 16 or over and responsible for at least one child, or
- aged 16 or over and disabled, or
- aged 25 or over and usually work at least 30 hours a week

WTC includes a basic element and a range of extra elements.

Retirement

The dictionary decries retirement as 'leaving one's job and stopping work, especially because one has reached a particular age.' Our culture promotes the goal of retirement and ceasing all labour to live a life filled with leisure. Is this a biblical goal?

Numbers 8:24-26 – the only reference to retirement in Scripture – applied specifically to the Levites working in the tabernacle. While people are physically and mentally capable, there is no scriptural basis for retiring and becoming unproductive – the concept of putting an older but able person 'out to pasture.' Don't let age stop you from finishing the work God has called you to accomplish. He will provide you with the necessary strength. For example, Moses was 80 years old when he began his 40-year adventure of leading the children of Israel.

The Bible does imply, however, that the type or intensity of work may change as we grow older – shifting gears to a less demanding pace to become more of an 'elder seated at the gate.' During this season of life we can use the experience and wisdom gained over a lifetime. If we have sufficient income to meet our needs apart from our jobs, we may choose to leave work to invest more time in serving others as God directs.

module three
My notes

What I learnt from studying work:

What I plan to do differently:

My other notes:

"Just as the rich rule the poor, so the borrower is servant to the lender"
(Proverbs 22:7, TLB)

module four
Debt

Debt is slavery

module four
Personal study

To be completed **prior to** module four meeting

Scripture to memorise
"Just as the rich rule the poor, so the borrower is servant to the lender"
(Proverbs 22:7, TLB)

Practical application
Continue with your spending tracker. In starting to look at debt please complete a debt schedule and review the notes and consider whether you should start repaying your debt using the snowball strategy. Please complete your debt repayment schedule(s).

Day one – let's review work
Read the work notes on pages 26-35 and answer:

1. What in the notes proved especially helpful or challenging? How will this impact you?

2. Do you usually recognise you are working for the Lord? If not, what could you do to be more aware that you work for Him?

Debt

Day two
Read Deuteronomy 15:7-8; 2 Kings 4:1 and Proverbs 27:1

1. What were some of the reasons for people being in debt in the Old Testament?

Read Deuteronomy 15:1-3

2. In the Old Testament what could the poor expect to happen to their debts?

3. What are the causes of debt today?

Day three
Read Romans 13:8; Proverbs 22:7 and 1 Corinthians 7:23

1. Why is debt discouraged in Scripture?

Romans 13:8:

Proverbs 22:7:

1 Corinthians 7:23:

2. How does this apply to you personally and, if you are in business, to your business?

3. If you are in debt, do you have a strategy to get out of debt? If you have a plan, what are your key milestones?

Day four
Read Psalm 37:21 and Proverbs 3:27-28

1. What do these verses say about debt repayment?

   Psalm 37:21:

   Proverbs 3:27-28:

2. Do you have debts where either of these principles need to be applied?

Day five
Read 2 Kings 4:1-7

1. What principles of getting out of debt can you identify from this passage?

2. Can you apply any of these principles to your present situation? How?

Day six
Read Proverbs 22:26-27 and Proverbs 17:18

1. What does the Bible say about guaranteeing* the debt of others?

*may also be referred to as cosigning, pledging or securing.

    Proverbs 22:26-27:

    Proverbs 17:18:

Read Proverbs 6:1-5

2. If someone has guaranteed a debt, what should he or she attempt to do?

☐ Please write your prayer requests in your prayer log before coming to the meeting.

module four
Crown notes

To be read after completing **module four** personal study

The amount of debt in our country has exploded — government debt, business debt and personal debt. Credit card and other unsecured debt has grown enormously. The average household with unsecured debt has more than £21,000. The average family works for more than 70 days a year just to pay interest.

In a recent year there were more than 100,000 individual insolvencies, including more than 40,000 Individual Voluntary Arrangements (IVAs). The average age of a bankrupt is someone in their early forties, while one fifth are under 30 years old. The loss of the family home as a result of increased repayment costs or the inability to pay the mortgage gives rise to significant distress within the home. Financial tension is often quoted as a contributory reason for divorce, and there are marriages that end largely because of financial problems and couples inability to communicate properly concerning them.

There seems to be an endless stream of advertisements and direct mail encouraging us to buy now and pay later. We are constantly bombarded with offers to take out credit cards, unsecured loans as well as CONsolidation loans. These loans seek to group together a number of debts with the almost inevitable result that more interest is ultimately paid. We all know that nothing about those monthly payments is easy. Advertisers fail to tell us the whole truth. They leave out one little word: debt.

What is debt?

The Oxford dictionary defines debt as 'a sum of money owed.' Debt includes bank loans, money borrowed from relatives, consumer loans, the home mortgage, money owed to credit card companies. Bills that become due in the month, such as any monthly account, e.g. window cleaning, are not considered debt provided they are paid on time. However, some utility bills may have an outstanding balance that is not covered by the ongoing monthly direct debits and, to that extent, there may be a debt rolled up into these accounts. This occurs when energy costs increase and there is no prompt action to increase the utility payments. One course of action here is to contact the utility company and revise payments for it is better to act sooner than later. If your utility bills are estimated, read your meter and update your supplier to ensure you are not taken unaware by an actual account that is higher than the estimate.

What debt really costs

We need to recognise the true cost of debt. Two common types of debt are credit card and the home mortgage. We will look initially at credit card debt.

Credit card debt
Please study the chart below:

1. Amount of interest you paid:				
Year 1	Year 10	Year 20	Year 30	Year 40
£1,000	£10,000	£20,000	£30,000	£40,000
2. What you would earn on £1,000 invested annually at 6 percent?				
Year 1	Year 10	Year 20	Year 30	Year 40
£30	£3,576	£17,888	£51,430	£119,405
3. How much could the lender earn from your payment at 18 percent?				
Year 1	Year 10	Year 20	Year 30	Year 40
£90	£15,638	£139,824	£832,133	£4,497,902

1. Assume you have £5,560 in credit card debt at an interest rate of 18 percent. This would cost about £1,000 in interest annually. Over 40 years the total interest payable would be £40,000

2. Look at line 2. As an alternative to paying interest, what would be the effect of saving £83.33 a month (£1,000 a year)? Over 40 years you would receive a return of £119,405, a return approaching 300 percent in addition to the £40,000 of your own capital, making a total investment of £159,405

3. Line 3 looks at what the lender earns at 18 percent. The lender's gross earnings from the interest at £83.33 interest a month amount to a staggering £4,497,902, a return of 11,245 percent

You can see what lenders have known for a long time – compounding interest has an incredible impact. It can work for you, or it can work against you. Is there any wonder credit card companies are eager for you to become one of their borrowers?

The other costs of debt
Debt often increases stress, which contributes to mental, physical, and emotional fatigue. It can stifle creativity and harm relationships. Many people raise their lifestyle through debt, only to discover that its burden then controls their lifestyle.

The Bible on debt

Scripture does not say that debt is a sin, but it discourages it. Remember, God loves us and has given us these principles for our benefit. Read the first portion of Romans 13:8 from several different translations: *"Owe no man any thing"* (KJV). *"Let no debt remain outstanding"* (NIV). *"Pay all your debts"* (TLB). *"Owe nothing to anyone"* (NASB). *"Keep out of debt and owe no man anything"* (AMP).

1. Debt is considered slavery

Proverbs 22:7 reads: *"just as the rich rule the poor, so the borrower is servant to the lender"* (TLB). When we are in debt, we're a servant to the lender. And the deeper we are in debt, the more like servants we become. We don't have the freedom to decide where to spend our income because it is already obligated to meet these debts.

In 1 Corinthians 7:23 (NLT), Paul writes *"God paid a high price for you, so don't be enslaved by the world."* Our Father made the ultimate sacrifice by giving His Son, the Lord Jesus Christ, to die for us. And He now wants His children free to serve Him rather than lenders.

2. Debt was considered a curse

In the Old Testament, being out of debt was one of the promised rewards for obedience.

"If you fully obey the Lord your God and carefully follow all his commands that I give you today, the Lord your God will set you high above all the nations on earth. All these blessings will come upon you and accompany you if you obey the Lord your God: The Lord will open the heavens, the storehouse of his bounty, to send rain on your land in season and to bless all the work of your hands. You will lend to many nations but will borrow from none."

Deuteronomy 28:1-2, 12

However, debt was one of the curses for disobedience.

"But it shall come to pass, if you do not obey the voice of the Lord your God, to observe carefully all His commandments and His statutes which I command you today, that all these curses will come upon you....The alien who is among you shall rise higher and higher above you, and you shall come down lower and lower. He shall lend to you, but you shall not lend to him; he shall be the head, and you shall be the tail."

Deuteronomy 28:15, 43-44, NKJV

3. Debt presumes upon tomorrow

When we get into debt, we assume that we will earn enough in the future to repay it. We plan for our jobs to continue or our investments to be profitable. The Bible cautions us against presumption: *"you who say, 'today or tomorrow we are going to a certain town and will stay there a year. We will do business there and make a profit.' How do you know what your life will be like tomorrow?...What you ought to say is, 'If the Lord wants us to, we will live and do this or that'"* (James 4:13-15, NLT).

Even when taking out a mortgage with a fixed term interest rate, there is the presumption that at the end of the term the interest rate will not increase significantly or that income will have increased to offset any additional mortgage payment due. In the case of a variable rate loan that is the presumption at the outset. When I was an accountant I learnt to counsel clients to make sure they could repay loans taking into account up to a two percent increase in interest rates.

4. Debt may deny God an opportunity

Ron Blue, an outstanding financial author and colleague, tells of a young man who wanted to go to Bible college to become a missionary. The young man had no money and thought the only way he could afford Bible college was to secure a student loan. However, this would have left him with £25,000 of debt by the time he graduated. He knew a missionary's salary would never be able to repay that much debt.

After a great deal of prayer, he decided to enroll without the aid of a loan, trusting God to meet his needs. He graduated without borrowing anything and grew in his appreciation for how God could provide his needs. This was the most valuable lesson learned in Bible college as he prepared for life on the mission field.

5. Debts can be cancelled and forgiven

Deuteronomy tells us that God's provision and a faithful, obedient people should mean that there are no poor in the land (Deuteronomy 15:4-5). But the same passage recognises that there will always be poor in the land (verse 11) and there are two implications. The first is that the people are instructed to lend freely to their neighbour (Deuteronomy 15:8) and this generosity in allowing others to borrow is a source of God's blessing. Secondly, every seven years all debts were to be cancelled (Deuteronomy 15:1-3) and that it was a selfish thought not to lend just before the cancellation of debts (verse 8). What can we learn? However trapped in debt we may be there is always hope. In our modern context this text does not permit people to borrow with no intent to repay. Nor, in principle, does it permit creditors to pursue repayments from those who cannot repay.

> As people begin to eliminate debt, the Lord blesses their faithfulness

Borrowing

The Bible is silent on when we can owe money. In our opinion it is permissible to owe money for a home mortgage, your business or vocation. This 'permissible debt' should meet four criteria.

- The item purchased is an asset with the potential to appreciate or produce an income
- The value of an item exceeds the amount owed against it
- The debt should not be so high that repayment puts undue strain on the spending plan
- The debt should not give rise to anxiety (Isaiah 32:17)

Here's how a home mortgage might qualify. Houses meet the first requirement since they usually appreciate. You can meet the second requirement by investing a reasonable deposit so that you could expect to sell the home for at least enough to repay the mortgage. The third requirement means buying an affordable house — one with a monthly repayment that doesn't strain your spending plan.

How long should it take to repay? That's between you and God, in my case it took 15 years instead of 20 years to repay. Many pensioners are today still in debt on their houses and are either having to work part-time, downsize or sell and rent.

Student debt

Student debt poses a specific problem and is one that students must address, with or without parental assistance. For most, student debt is almost inevitable for those wishing to obtain a degree. In fact student debt is a particular type of debt. You will never secure a loan at such a low rate of interest nor one in which the repayments are directly linked to earnings. That said, it is still a burden of debt on people at the start of their adult lives. There is the danger that it creates in young people a culture of debt, an acceptance that focuses on stretching to borrow the maximum according to affordability.

How to get out of debt

Start by making a decision that you will not go one penny more in debt. Increasing debt has to stop and now is the time to make that decision.

Then consider these nine steps for getting out of debt. The steps are easy, but following them requires discipline. Your goal is Debt Free Day – when you become absolutely free of debt.

1. Pray

In 2 Kings 4:1-7, we read about a widow who was threatened with losing her sons to her creditor. When she asked Elisha for help, he told her to borrow many empty jars from her neighbours. Then God multiplied her only possession – a small amount of oil – until all the jars were filled. She sold the oil and paid her debts to free her children.

The same God who provided supernaturally for the widow is interested in freeing you from debt. The first step is to pray. Seek God's help and guidance in your journey toward Debt Free Day. He may act immediately or slowly over time. In either case, prayer is essential. A trend is emerging. As people begin to eliminate debt, the Lord blesses their faithfulness. Even if you can afford only a small monthly repayment of your debt, please do it. God can multiply your efforts.

2. Sell what you are not using

Evaluate your possessions to determine whether you should sell any of them to help you get out of debt more quickly. What about the bike you no longer use? That set of golf clubs gathering dust? Is there anything you can sell to help you get out of debt?

3. Establish a written budget

Your Practical Application Workbook will enable you to develop your own personal budget. This budget will help you plan ahead as you analyse your spending patterns to see where you can minimise outgoings. It will be an effective bridle on impulse spending.

4. The snowball strategy

How do you 'snowball' yourself out of debt?

> **"Godliness...is a means of great gain when accompanied by contentment"**

- **Pay off your smallest credit card debt.** Review your credit card debts. In addition to making the minimum payments on all your cards, focus on accelerating the payment of your smallest high-interest credit card first. You will be encouraged as you make progress, finally eliminating that debt.

- **After you pay off the first credit card, apply its payment toward the next smallest one.** After the second card is paid off, apply what you were paying on the first and second toward the third smallest credit card, and so forth. That's the snowball strategy in action!

- **Pay off your smallest consumer debt.** After you have paid off all your credit cards, focus on paying off your consumer debts in exactly the same way as you wiped out your plastic. Make the minimum payments on any of your store card debts, but focus on accelerating the payment of your smallest higher-interest store card debt first. Then, after you pay off the first store card debt, apply its payment toward the next smallest one. After the second one is paid off, apply what you were paying on the first and second to pay off the third, and so forth until you have repaid your credit card and store card debts and then you can start repaying your unsecured and other debts.

5. Consider earning additional income

Many people hold jobs that simply do not pay enough to allow them to pay off their debts quickly enough. A temporary part-time job can make a huge difference to how quickly you reach Debt Free Day.

6. Control the use of the 'plastic'

A wave of credit card offers is overwhelming our post. Many of these entice us with low teaser rates that rise to high levels within a few months. Credit cards are not sinful, but they are dangerous.

One way to limit the temptation of additional cards and to make meal time more peaceful is to opt out of receiving telemarketing calls and pre-approved credit card offers by mail. To do this register with the telephone and mail preference services. These are central opt out services where you can register your wish not to receive unsolicited calls or mailings. Their contact information can be found on their websites.

When people use credit cards rather than cash, they spend about one-third more because it doesn't feel like real money; it's just plastic. As one shopper said to another "I like credit cards lots more than money, because they go so much further!" If you don't pay the entire credit card balance within two months, you may need to perform some plastic surgery – any good scissors will do!

7. Be content with what you have

Advertisers use powerful methods to get us to buy. Frequently the message is intended to foster discontentment with what we have. An example is the American company that opened a new plant in Central America because the labour was relatively inexpensive. Everything went well until the villagers received their first pay cheque; afterward they did not return to work. Several days later, the manager went down to the village chief to determine the cause of this problem. The chief responded "why should we work? We already have everything we need." The plant stood idle for two months until someone came up with the idea of sending a mail-order catalogue to every villager. There has not been an employment problem since!

Note these three realities of our consumer-driven economy:

- The more television you watch or surfing the Internet you do, the more you spend
- The more you look at catalogues and magazines, the more you spend
- The more you shop, the more you spend.

> **Avoid the trap**
>
> One bar maid living in London accumulated £30,000 of store card debt. Her income? £1,000 a month – gross.

There is an interesting passage in 1 Timothy 6:5-6: *"men of corrupt mind, who have been robbed of the truth and who think that godliness is a means to financial gain. But godliness with contentment is great gain."* When we are content with what we have and wait to buy until we can do it using cash – that is great gain.

8. Consider a radical change in lifestyle

A growing number of people have lowered their standard of living significantly to get out of debt more quickly. In order to achieve this some have downsized their homes, rented apartments or moved in with family members. Others have sold cars with large monthly payments and have bought inexpensive ones for cash. In short, they have temporarily sacrificed their standard of living so they could 'snowball' to pay off their debt more quickly.

9. Do not give up!

The last step may be the most difficult. On October 29, 1941, Winston Churchill, made a speech. World War II was devastating Europe, and England's fate was in doubt. Churchill stood and said "never give in. Never give in. Never, never, never, never – in nothing, great or small, large or petty – never give in except to convictions of honour and good sense."

Never give up in your effort to get out of debt. It may require hard work and sacrifice, but the freedom is worth the struggle.

> **How would it feel to have no debt or repayments of any kind?**

Escaping the car debt trap

Car debt is one of the biggest obstacles for most people on their journey to biblical financial freedom because most people never get out of it. Just when they are ready to pay off a car, they trade it in and purchase a newer one with more credit.

Unlike a home, which usually appreciates in value, the moment you drive a car from the sales forecourt it depreciates in value. It's worth less than you paid for it.

Take these three steps to get out of car debt:

1. Decide to keep your car at least three years longer than your car loan and pay off your car loan
2. After your last payment, keep making the payment, but pay it to yourself. Put it into an account that you will use to buy your next car
3. When you are ready to replace your car, the cash you have saved plus your car's trade-in value should be sufficient to buy a car without credit. It may not be a new car, but a newer low-mileage used car without any debt is better value anyway

The home mortgage

If you own a home or plan to purchase one in the future, we want to encourage you to pay it off more rapidly than scheduled.

Rhoda and I had said our goodbyes to Ted and as we looked at each other knew that we needed to focus on clearing our mortgage as soon as possible. In many respects this was something of a dream, but we were determined to share our plans with our church leadership.

Understanding the numbers

Every mortgage comes with a payment schedule based on the length of the loan and the interest rate. Knowing how this works will help you develop a plan for paying off the mortgage. Let's examine the payment schedule of a mortgage. In the following example, we are assuming a £100,000 mortgage at a 7 percent fixed interest rate, over 25 years. The first year looks like this:

Payment schedule

Payment	Month	Payment	Interest	Principal	Balance
1	Jan	706.78	583.33	123.45	99876.55
2	Feb	706.78	582.61	124.17	99752.38
3	Mar	706.78	581.89	124.89	99627.49
4	Apr	706.78	581.16	125.62	99501.87
5	May	706.78	580.43	126.35	99375.52
6	June	706.78	579.69	127.09	99248.43
7	July	706.78	578.95	127.83	99120.60
8	Aug	706.78	578.20	128.58	98992.02
9	Sep	706.78	577.45	129.33	98862.69
10	Oct	706.78	576.70	130.08	98732.61
11	Nov	706.78	575.94	130.84	98601.77
12	Dec	706.78	575.18	131.60	98470.17
Totals for the year:		8481.36	6951.53	1529.83	

As you can see, during the early years of the mortgage almost all the payments go to pay the interest. Of a total £8,481.36 in house payments made during the first year, only £1,529.83 went toward the loan reduction. In fact, it will be more than 15 years before the principal and the interest portions of the payment equal each other. I don't know about you, but a 25-year goal to pay off my home mortgage doesn't excite me. If this can be reduced to 15 years, then the goal becomes more attainable.

How to pay off the mortgage more quickly

There are several ways to accelerate the payment of your home mortgage.

1. Reduce the length of the mortgage

One method of reducing the interest is to reduce the length of the loan period while another is to take advantage of any increased monthly payment you are allowed to make under your mortgage agreement. Many mortgage agreements allow additional monthly payments of up to 10 percent of the repayment.

With the example on the previous page, the total interest payable over 25 years is £112,033.76. If the monthly payments were increased to £775.30 the loan would be repaid in 20 years. You will have paid an additional £16,444.80, but the total interest would reduce to £86,071.74, a reduction of £25,962.02 or almost 25 percent less. Furthermore, you will no longer have the remaining monthly payments to make, which under the 25 year mortgage would have amounted to £42,406.80.

Let's also compare a £120,000, 25-year mortgage at 7 percent and a 15-year mortgage at 7 percent.

Mortgage: £120,000	25 Years	15 Years
Monthly payment	£848	£1,078
At the end of fifteen years:		
Interest paid	£105,711	£74,147
Principal paid	£46,953	£120,000
Principal balance due	£73,047	£0 (Yes!)
Interest paid, years 16–25	£60,294	£0
Total interest paid	**£134,441**	**£74,147**

If you can shrink the duration of your mortgage in half, the interest savings are huge.

2. Add something to the required payment

Many mortgages allow a prepayment of up to 10 percent of the monthly repayments. If you wish to increase your repayments more than this you will need to check with your mortgage provider and/or seek professional advice. We made sure we reduced the term of our mortgage by taking out a new mortgage when we moved home and contracting for a mortgage with a shorter term. Interest rate increases on mortgages toward the end of the first decade of the millennium caused many home owners to regret taking out the maximum mortgage on a low interest fixed rate 'prime loan.'

3. Bonuses

Finally, when you receive an employment-related bonus or an unexpected gift, give generously to God and then consider applying the rest to repaying your debts. If such sums are applied to reducing home debt each time it occurs it will have a significant impact on paying off your mortgage.

I know several people who saved their entire one-off gifts and bonuses and have then moved home and used all this money to significantly reduce their next mortgage.

There are traditionally two primary arguments against prepaying a mortgage. (1) Why pay off a low-interest home mortgage – you can earn more elsewhere? (2) With inflation, your later payments are made with less valuable pounds.

For these reasons repaying the mortgage early has not been perceived as wise. However, the Bible discourages debt. We simply challenge you to seek Christ with an open heart to learn what He wants you to do.

When talking to people in debt I often find them near the point of desperation, unable to see a way out of their situation. Sometimes the debt has been through no apparent fault of their own and on occasions debt had become so normal that the scale of the debt and the manipulation of repayments commonplace. Those in debt are often in denial about their situation, or alternatively accept it as normal. Paul reminds us that 'God's ways are not our ways.' I cannot think of one person who having become debt free didn't resolve to never let it happen again.

Becoming debt free was a major step towards Rhoda and I being free to serve God in Crown. What a joy to be able to serve in this way and not be a slave to debt. Being conformed to the ways of this world can include being trapped in the world's financial system. Let us be conformed to God's ways so that we can be freer to serve Him.

Having read this, how would it feel to have no debt and no payments of any kind including your home mortgage? We can tell you from experience, it feels great!

If you want to pay off your mortgage, it is a good idea to discuss this with your lender to establish what is possible, and to arrange a new repayment schedule, to ensure proper crediting of your prepayment.

Investment debt

Should you borrow money to make an investment? In our opinion, it is permissible to borrow for an investment, but a borrower should seek to limit the security for the loan to the asset itself. Therefore it would be wise not to guarantee the loan beyond the security offered by the investment. In practice, the liability to the loan remains, unless it is borrowed through a limited company and no personal guarantee is given.

Because of the seeming inevitability of difficult financial circumstances – like the 'credit crunch' that started in the US in 2007 and rippled through to the UK until it appeared like a full-blown hurricane in 2008 – it is always wise to limit risk given the possibility of an uncertain marketplace.

It is, in our opinion, unwise to borrow all the funds required to make an investment. You should always have a stake in any investment and it is wise to build up that stake rather than seek to cash in any other assets to fund your initial stake.

With all your investment decisions, taking appropriate qualified advice counsel is essential. I do not however believe it is wise or godly to borrow money to speculate, e.g. to buy stocks and shares.

Business debt

We also want to encourage you to pray about becoming debt free in your business. Many business owners are recognising the competitive advantage and increased stability they have when they eliminate business debt.

As a business adviser, I have assisted many businesses raise finance for their business plans. I have assisted those who have made millions and, sadly, seen many suffer as a result of having borrowed against unrealistic expectations. Sometimes people lose their money, or money they have borrowed, through no immediate fault of their own. It is essential to seek good counsel when borrowing, recognising that those lending are not impartial and their advice should be considered alongside other counsel.

Here is our rule of thumb on business debt: use as little as possible and pay it off as quickly as possible.

Church debt

Scripture does not specifically address whether a church may borrow money to build or expand its premises. In our opinion, such debt is permissible if the church leadership clearly senses the Lord leading to do so. If a church borrows, we recommend that it raise as much money as possible for the deposit and establish a plan to pay off the debt as rapidly as possible. A growing number of churches have chosen to build without the use of any debt. For many of these churches, the members have been encouraged and their faith increased as they have observed God providing the necessary funds.

Repayment responsibilities

Prompt payment

Many people delay paying creditors until payments are overdue, even when they have the money. This, however, is not biblical. Proverbs 3:27-28 reads *"do not withhold good from those who deserve it, when it is in your power to act. Do not say to your neighbour, Come back later; I'll give it tomorrow – when you now have it with you."*

Godly people should pay their debts and bills as promptly as they can. Some try to pay each bill the same day they receive it to demonstrate to others that knowing Jesus Christ has made them financially responsible.

Using your savings

Very few families would survive without going into debt if there was no income for two months. For this reason, it is always important to have a savings reserve. If you do not have any emergency savings start by working out how you can set aside one week's income as savings, then build to four weeks or a month and finally plan to have up to three months' income set aside in savings. These funds are available for emergencies, such as the need to replace a household appliance or an unexpected car bill and will ensure that your finances do not fall apart.

Bankruptcy

A court can declare people bankrupt and unable to pay their debts. Depending on the type of bankruptcy, the court will either allow them to develop a plan to repay their creditors or it will distribute their property among the creditors as payment.

Should a godly person declare bankruptcy? Generally, no. Psalm 37:21 (RSV) tells us *"the wicked borrows, and cannot pay back, but the righteous is generous and gives."*

However, in our opinion, bankruptcy is permissible under three circumstances:

- Where a creditor forces a person into bankruptcy
- When the borrower experiences such extreme financial difficulties that there is no option. There are occasions when bankruptcy is the only viable option when the financial challenges become too extreme to reverse. That option needs to be exercised only after all others have been explored

- If the emotional health of the borrower is at stake. If the debtor's emotional health is at stake because of inability to cope with the pressure of aggressive creditors, bankruptcy can be an option

Declaring bankruptcy should not be a cavalier decision, because it normally remains on a credit report for six years, and it often impairs the ability to obtain future credit at reasonable interest rates. Potential employers and landlords are also likely to learn of a past bankruptcy. It can haunt people for some time, and although it provides relief, it is not exactly the fresh start that some advertise.

Guaranteeing

Please use sound judgement and never guarantee

Guaranteeing relates to debt. Anytime you guarantee, you become legally responsible for the debt of another. It is just as if you went to the bank, borrowed the money and gave it to your friend or relative who is asking you to guarantee. In effect, you promise to pay back the entire amount if the borrower does not.

Fortunately, Scripture gives us clear direction about guaranteeing. Proverbs 17:18 says *"it is poor judgement to countersign another's note, to become responsible for his debts"* (TLB). The words "poor judgement" are literally translated "destitute of mind!"

A parent often acts as a guarantor for his or her child's car and sometimes their first home; we decided not to do this. We wanted to model for our children the importance of not guaranteeing and to discourage them from using debt. Instead, we trained them to think ahead and save for the cash purchase of their first cars and home.

If you have already guaranteed a loan, the Scripture gives you counsel. Proverbs 6:1-5 says *"son, if you endorse a note for someone you hardly know, guaranteeing his debt, you are in serious trouble. You may have trapped yourself by your agreement. Quick! Get out of it if you possibly can! Swallow your pride; don't let embarrassment stand in the way. Go and beg to have your name erased. Don't put it off....If you can get out of this trap you have saved yourself like a deer that escapes from a hunter, or a bird from the net"* (TLB).

Please use sound judgement and never guarantee unless a guarantee is a mandatory requirement for a son or daughter (e.g. a university accommodation guarantee).

Credit report and score

Everyone should get a copy of their credit report once every 12 months. Your credit score determines whether you can get credit. And your score may be high enough to get credit but not high enough to get a decent interest rate – whether you're looking for a mortgage, a credit card, a car loan or some other type of credit. Without good scores, your application to rent accommodation may be turned down. Your scores can affect your car insurance premiums and in some cases even getting a job.

The primary things that will harm your credit score are late payments or non-payments of bills or debts, bankruptcy, foreclosure, repossession, bills or loans sent for collection. Your credit score will also be affected if your credit history is short, or if you are up to your maximum credit limits. To improve your credit score, the two most important actions you can take are to pay your bills on time and to reduce your total debt. Once you start doing this, your score will begin to improve in about three months.

module four
My notes

What I learnt from studying debt:

What I plan to do differently:

My other notes:

"The way of a fool seems right to him, but a wise man listens to advice"
(Proverbs 12:15)

module five
Counsel

A wise person seeks advice

module five
Personal study

To be completed **prior to** module five meeting

Scripture to memorise
"The way of a fool seems right to him, but a wise man listens to advice"
(Proverbs 12:15)

Practical application
This is budgeting week one. This week you will complete your spending tracker and prepare your spending budget. Please prepare your spending budget after reviewing the five budget tests. Aside from looking at numbers please review 'my life goals.'

Day one – let's review debt
Read the debt notes on pages 42-53 and answer:

1. Are you in debt? If so, what steps do you sense God wants you to take to become free of debt?

2. What did you learn about debt that proved to be especially helpful?

Counsel

Day two
Read Proverbs 12:15; Proverbs 13:10 and Proverbs 15:22

1. What are some of the benefits of seeking counsel?

Proverbs 12:15:

Proverbs 13:10:

Proverbs 15:22:

2. What are some of the benefits you have experienced from seeking counsel (of any description)?

3. What gets in the way of you seeking counsel?

Day three
Read Psalm 16:7 and Psalm 32:8

1. What do we learn about how God provides counsel?

Read Psalm 106:13-15

2. In this passage, what was the consequence of not seeking the Lord's counsel?

3. Have you ever suffered for not seeking God's counsel? If so, describe what happened.

Day four
Read Psalm 119:24; Psalm 119:66; Psalm 119:105; 2 Timothy 3:16-17 and Hebrews 4:12

1. Give several reasons why the Bible should serve as your counsellor.

Read Psalm 119:11(b) and Psalm 119:98-100

2. Living by the counsel of Scripture gives us rewards that:

   Help us not sin against:

   Makes us wiser than:

   Gives us more insight than:

   Gives us more understanding than:

3. Do you consistently read and study the Bible? If not, what gets in the way?

Read Psalm 119:7-11

4. How can you keep your heart pure?

5. What does it mean to hide God's Word? What is the consequence?

___

Day five
Read Proverbs 1:8-9

1. Who should be among your counsellors?

2. In your opinion, who should be the number-one human counsellor of a husband? Of a wife? Of a single person? Why?

Read Proverbs 11:14 and Ecclesiastes 4:9-12

3. What do the following verses communicate to you?

Proverbs 11:14:

Ecclesiastes 4:9-12:

4. How could you apply this principle in your personal and/or business life?

Day six
Read Psalm 1:1-3

1. Who should you avoid as a counsellor?

2. What should you seek in a good counsellor?

3. What is your definition of a wicked person?

Read Proverbs 12:5

4. In what circumstance might you consider input of a person who does not know Christ? If so, when?

☐ **Please write your prayer requests in your prayer log before coming to the meeting.**

module five
Crown notes

To be read after completing **module five** personal study

I frequently counsel people with financial problems. Often they could have avoided their difficulties if only they had sought counsel from someone with a solid understanding of God's way of handling money.

Seeking counsel

Two attitudes keep us from seeking counsel. The first one is pride. Our culture perceives seeking advice as a sign of weakness. We are told "stand on your own two feet. You don't need anyone to help make your decisions for you!" Advertisers subtly encourage this because they know that the impulse sale is often lost when the purchaser takes time to seek counsel.

The second attitude is stubbornness, characterised by the statement "don't confuse me with the facts. My mind is already made up!" We often resist seeking counsel because we do not want to expose the financial facts another person might discover. We don't want to be told we can't afford what we already have decided to buy.

God encourages us to use a great gift He has provided for our benefit – godly counsellors. In Proverbs 19:20 we read *"listen to advice and accept instruction, and in the end you will be wise."* Proverbs 12:15 says *"the way of a fool seems right to him, but a wise man listens to advice."* And Proverbs 10:8 says *"the wise man is glad to be instructed, but a self-sufficient fool falls flat on his face"* (TLB).

We seek counsel to secure insights, suggestions and alternatives that will aid in making a proper decision. It is not the counsellor's role to make the decision; we retain that responsibility.

Gather facts, but…

We need to assemble the facts that will influence our decisions, but we also need to seek God's direction as well. Sometimes He directs in a way contrary to our assessment of the facts alone.

This is illustrated in Numbers 13 and 14. Moses sent 12 spies into the Promised Land. They all returned with an identical evaluation of the facts: it was a prosperous land inhabited by terrifying giants. Only two of the 12 spies, Joshua and Caleb, understood God wanted them to go in and possess the Promised Land. Because the children of Israel relied only on the facts and did not act in faith on what the Lord wanted for them, they suffered 40 years of wandering in the wilderness until that entire generation died.

If you are married, the first person you need to consult is your spouse

Sources of counsel

What are the sources of counsel we need to seek? Before making a financial decision, particularly an important one, subject it to three sources of counsel.

The counsel of Scripture

First, what does God's Word say about a particular issue? The psalmist wrote *"your laws are both my light and my counsellors"* (Psalm 119:24, TLB).

"Your commands make me wiser than my enemies....I have more insight than all my teachers, for I meditate on your statutes....I have more understanding than the elders, for I obey your precepts."
Psalm 119:98-100

When we think of those who are skilled in financial decision making, we often think of accountants, Independent Financial Advisors (IFAs) or those who are older and more experienced. Yet the Bible offers us more insight and wisdom than financial experts who do not know God's way of handling money. I would rather obey the truth of Scripture than risk suffering the consequences of following my own inclinations or the opinions of people.

The Bible makes this remarkable claim about itself: *"for the word of God is living and active. Sharper than any double-edged sword...it judges the thoughts and attitudes of the heart"* (Hebrews 4:12). The truths in the Bible are timeless. It is the only book that God ever wrote and it is our manufacturer's handbook. The Bible communicates God's counsel and direction.

Were you surprised to learn that the Bible contains 2,350 verses dealing with how we should handle money and possessions? It is the very first filter through which we should run decisions. If it answers the question, we do not have to go any further because the Bible contains God's written, revealed will.

> If the Bible provides clear direction in a financial matter, we know what to do

Jonathan and Helen were faced with an uncomfortable decision. Helen's brother and his wife had just moved to Bristol from Surrey. Because they had experienced financial difficulties and been through an Independent Voluntary Arrangement the bank would not lend them the necessary funds for the mortgage unless they had someone to act as guarantor. They asked Jonathan and Helen to do so. Helen pleaded with Jonathan to do so; however, he was reluctant.

A friend referred them to the verses that warn against acting as a guarantor. After reading the passages, Helen said "who am I to argue with God? We shouldn't act as guarantor." Jonathan was tremendously relieved.

Two years later, Helen's brother and his wife were divorced, and he declared bankruptcy. Can you imagine the strain on their marriage if Jonathan had acted as guarantor? He might have said "Helen, I can't believe your brother did this! You got me into this! I tried not to act as guarantor but you forced me!" They probably would not have been able to survive financially.

If the Bible provides clear direction in a financial matter, we know what to do. If the Bible is not specific about an issue, we should subject our decision to the second source of counsel: godly people.

The counsel of godly people

"The godly man is a good counsellor because he is just and fair and knows right from wrong" (Psalm 37:30-31, TLB). The Christian life is not one of independence from other Christians but of interdependence on one other. This is illustrated clearly in Paul's discussion concerning the body of Christ in 1 Corinthians 12. Each of us is pictured as a different member of this body. Our ability to function most effectively is dependent on the members working together. God has given each of us certain abilities and gifts, but God has not given any one person all the abilities that he or she needs to be most productive.

Spouse

If you are married, the first person you need to consult is your spouse. Although I have been trained financially I greatly value my wife's financial perspective and counsel. Financial decisions involve far more than numbers and her counsel and good housekeeping have saved us a great deal of money. If you have a spouse, make sure you maximise this advantage in your relationship.

Women tend to be gifted with a wonderfully sensitive and intuitive nature that is usually very accurate. Men tend to focus more objectively on the facts. The husband and wife need each other to achieve the proper balance for a correct decision. I believe that these attributes are important and add an important dimension to marriage. Many times God communicates most clearly to the husband through his wife.

In many relationships one partner is much better at managing personal finance than the other. It is important for the other partner to recognise this but also to work together in managing personal finance. Regardless of your spouse's business education or financial aptitude you must cultivate and seek his or her counsel. You may feel that you have the business background, the financial skills but your partner may have or can develop excellent business and financial skills and their insight will always enrich your own.

> **If you are married, the first person you need to consult is your spouse**

- **It will enhance your relationship!** The husband and wife should agree, because they both will experience the consequences of the decision. Even if their choice proves to be disastrous, their relationship remains intact. There are no grounds for an 'I told you so' response.

- **It honours your spouse.** Unfortunately, some in our culture do not feel valuable. Seeking your spouse's counsel will help enormously in the development of healthy and proper self-esteem. When a husband or wife seeks the other's advice, he or she actually is communicating 'I love you. I respect you. I value your insight.'

- **It prepares your spouse for the future.** Consistently asking for advice also keeps your spouse informed of your true financial condition. This is important in the event you predecease your spouse or are unable to work. Planning for death isn't everyone's activity of first choice. However, I have seen many families having to cope with financial disarray and lack of financial awareness after the death of a loved one who had sole responsibility for the finances. Involving one another in home finances is important, especially as there is usually one partner for whom this is not an area of natural gifting.

Parents

The second source of counsel is our parents.

"My son, keep your father's commands and do not forsake your mother's teaching. Bind them upon your heart for ever; fasten them around your neck. When you walk, they will guide you; when you sleep, they will watch over you; when you awake, they will speak to you."

Proverbs 6:20-22

Our parents have the benefit of years of experience and they know us well. In our opinion, we should seek their counsel even if they do not yet know Christ or have not been wise money managers themselves. Over the years, it's not uncommon for a barrier to be erected between a child and parents. Asking their advice is a way to honour our parents and to build a bridge. It is a compliment, an expression of admiration, for anyone to ask your advice. A word of caution: although the husband and wife should seek the counsel of their parents, the advice of the parents should be subordinate to the advice of the spouse, especially if a family conflict materializes.

  "A man will leave his father and mother and be united to his wife, and they will become one flesh" (Genesis 2:24).

Experienced people

We should also consult people experienced in the area in which we are attempting to make a decision. If you are considering an investment in property, locate the most qualified property agent to advise you. If you want to purchase a car, first ask a trustworthy mechanic to examine it and give you an opinion.

A multitude of counsellors

We read in Proverbs 15:22 *"plans fail for lack of counsel, but with many advisers they succeed."* And Proverbs 11:14 says *"for lack of guidance a nation falls, but many advisers make victory sure."*

  Another practical way of gaining counsel is to be involved with a mentoring group or to have people around you whose counsel you can seek. When building my businesses I always sought out those whose counsel I knew I could trust, and that included my church leaders. Similarly, I have important relationships with Christians who I can turn to for wisdom and advice. I meet regularly with these men who have over the years been able to question and guide me through when times have been challenging. There were times when I was struggling with problems in my business and I kept waking in the middle of the night unable to get back to sleep because of worry. It is good to be able to turn to people who love you and give objective counsel, even if it hurts.

  We are more receptive to constructive criticism when it comes from someone who cares for us.

"A cord of three strands is not quickly broken"

We also have learned that a major advantage of this close relationship is knowing each other's weaknesses and strengths. This knowledge improves our discernment and counsel. Solomon describes the benefits of interdependence upon one another:

"Two are better than one, because they have a good return for their work. If one falls down, his friend can help him up. But pity the man who falls and has no-one to help him up! Also, if two lie down together, they will keep warm. But how can one keep warm alone? Though one may be overpowered, two can defend themselves. A cord of three strands is not quickly broken."

Ecclesiastes 4:9-12

It can be very productive to gather your counsellors together because the suggestions of one will trigger insights from another and clear direction often emerges.

When seeking a multitude of counsellors, don't expect them all to offer the same recommendations. They may even disagree sharply, but a common thread usually develops. Other times, each counsellor may supply a different insight you need to help you make the decision. We encourage you to include your pastor among your counsellors, particularly when you face a major decision.

Throughout Scripture we are encouraged to wait on the Lord

The counsel of the Lord

During the process of analysing the facts, searching the Bible and obtaining the counsel of godly people, we need to seek direction from the Lord and His Word. This is the most important thing we can do. In Isaiah 9:6 we are told that one of God's names is "Wonderful Counsellor."

The Psalms also identify God as our counsellor. *"I (the Lord) will instruct you and teach you the way you should go; I will counsel you with my eye upon you"* (Psalm 32:8, RSV). *"You (the Lord) guide me with your counsel, and afterwards you will take me into glory"* (Psalm 73:24). *"I will praise the Lord, who counsels me"* (Psalm 16:7).

The Bible contains numerous examples of the unfortunate consequences of not seeking God's counsel as well as the blessings of heeding His counsel. After the children of Israel began their campaign to capture the Promised Land, some of the natives (Gibeonites) attempted to enter into a peace treaty with Israel. The Gibeonites deceived the leaders of Israel into believing they were from a distant land. Joshua 9:14-15 reads *"the men of Israel sampled their (Gibeonites') provisions but did not enquire of the Lord. Then Joshua made a treaty of peace with them to let them live, and the leaders of the assembly ratified it by oath."*

The consequence of not seeking the Lord's counsel was that the Promised Land remained populated with ungodly people and Israel became ensnared by their false gods. The leaders were influenced by the 'facts' they could see – facts that were designed to deceive them into thinking that the Gibeonites lived far away. In many situations, only God can reveal truth and proper direction. Only He knows the future and the ultimate outcome of a decision.

Throughout Scripture we are encouraged to wait on the Lord. Whenever you feel hurried or pressured or confused concerning a decision, go to a quiet place that will allow you to listen for His still, small voice. The world around you screams 'hurry!' but our loving heavenly Father's advice is worth waiting for.

Counsel to avoid

Avoiding the counsel of the wicked

We need to avoid one particular source of counsel. *"How blessed is the man who does not walk in the counsel of the wicked"* (Psalm 1:1). The word 'blessed' literally means to be 'happy many times over.' The word 'wicked' is a strong word and is often used to describe people who behave in an extremely cruel manner. The former Iraqi dictator was often described by the media as wicked. The dictionary widens the use of the term to include those who are sinful or iniquitous, while the first three synonyms on dictionary.com are unrighteous, ungodly and godless. Thus the definition of a 'wicked' person is one who lives without regard to God. A wicked person can be one who does not yet personally know the Lord or one who knows Jesus Christ as Saviour but is not following Him in obedience. Avoid the counsel of the wicked.

There are people who would advise us to do things that are wrong or would take advantage of us in financial matters for their advantage. We need discernment. If anything sounds too good to be true it probably is!

In my opinion, if there is no suitably qualified Christian, then technical or professional advice should be sought from those you deem to be qualified to advise. Armed with that advice, our financial decision should be based on prayer and possibly a second opinion from those who know the Lord.

Fortune tellers, mediums, and spiritualists

The Bible clearly forbids seeking the advice of fortune tellers, mediums, or spiritualists: *"do not turn to mediums or seek out spiritists, for you will be defiled by them. I am the Lord your God"* (Leviticus 19:31). Study this next passage carefully: *"Saul died because he was unfaithful to the Lord; he did not keep the word of the Lord, and even consulted a medium for guidance, and did not enquire of the Lord. So the Lord put him to death"* (1 Chronicles 10:13-14). Saul died, in part, because he went to a medium. We should also avoid anything they use in forecasting the future, such as horoscopes and all other practices of the occult.

Biased counsel

We need to be cautious of biased counsel – that which is not impartial or independent. When receiving financial advice, ask yourself these questions: "What stake does this person have in the outcome of my decision? Does he or she stand to gain or lose from this decision?" If the advisor will profit, be cautious when evaluating this counsel and always seek a second, unbiased opinion.

Your questions

Q: How often should my husband and I review our spending plan?

A: Meet at least once a week to pray, review your financial progress, and celebrate the victories. Use this as an opportunity to grow closer together as a couple.

A word to the counselled

When you are seeking advice, supply your counsellor with all the important facts. Do not attempt to manipulate your advisor to give the answer you want by concealing information.

Major decisions

Whenever you face a major decision such as a job change or house purchase, it is very helpful to go to a quiet place where you can spend uninterrupted time praying, reading Scripture and seeking God's direction. We encourage you to consider fasting during this time.

Know your counsellors

Be selective in choosing your counsellors. Include those who are gifted with wisdom. *"He who walks with the wise grows wise"* (Proverbs 13:20). Make sure they have the courage to give you advice that may be contrary to your wishes.

Continually ask God for wisdom. *"If any of you lack wisdom, let him ask of God, that giveth to all men liberally…and it shall be given him. But let him ask in faith, nothing wavering"* (James 1:5-6, KJV).

As you seek counsel, do not be surprised if the answer comes out of your own mouth. Interacting with others allows you to verbalise thoughts and feelings that you may never have expressed clearly.

A word to counsellors

Counselling others can be a frustrating experience if you misunderstand the proper role of the counsellor. Simply stated, counsellors should lovingly communicate their understanding of the truth and then leave the results to God. When I was younger I sometimes made the mistake of becoming involved emotionally in whether people would act on my recommendations. I discovered that some people were not prepared to follow advice. On some occasions, I later discovered that my counsel was flawed. Counsellors need to be content, knowing that the Lord is in control of every counselling experience.

Observe strict confidentiality

The person seeking advice needs to know that nothing he or she says will be communicated to another person without permission. Only in an environment of trust will there be the candid dialogue that produces successful results.

When you do not know

When you do not know the answer to a question, be careful not to fabricate one. Simply respond: 'I do not know.' Often people come with problems or circumstances that are outside of our experience. The best way to serve is to refer them to someone who has expertise in their area of need.

module five
My notes

What I learnt from studying counsel:

What I plan to do differently:

My other notes:

module five
My notes

> **"I have learned to be content whatever the circumstances. I know what it is to be in need, and I know what it is to have plenty...I can do everything through him who gives me strength."**
> **(Philippians 4:11-13)**

module six
Lifestyle

Exercise wisdom when you spend

module six
Personal study

To be completed **prior to** module six meeting

Scripture to memorise
"I have learned to be content whatever the circumstances. I know what it is to be in need, and I know what it is to have plenty...I can do everything through him who gives me strength" (Philippians 4:11-13)

Practical application
Week two of budgeting. Please begin your spending plan and look at how you record your spending, including your bank, cash and credit card records. This will involve reconciling your bank and 'plastic' accounts to your records and linking them to your spending plan.

Day one – let's review counsel
Read the counsel notes on pages 60-66 and answer:

1. What elements of God's perspective on counsel especially interested you?

2. From whom would you actively seek counsel when faced with a major financial decision? If you have no one, whose counsel do you propose to seek in the future?

Lifestyle

Day two
Read Deuteronomy 30:15-16; Joshua 1:8 and Hebrews 11:36-40

1. What do each of these passages communicate to you about financial prosperity?

   Deuteronomy 30:15-16:

Joshua 1:8:

Hebrews 11:36-40:

Reflect on the lives of Job (Job 1:8-21); Joseph (Genesis 37:23-28; 39:7-20) and Paul (2 Corinthians 11:23-27)

2. Did they ever experience periods of financial abundance and at other times a lack of financial prosperity?

3. Was their lack of financial prosperity a result of sin or lack of faith?

4. Should all Christians prosper financially? Why?

Read Psalm 73:1-20

5. What does this passage tell you about the prosperity of the wicked?

Day three
Read Philippians 4:11-13 and 1 Timothy 6:6-8

1. What do these passages say about contentment?

Philippians 4:11-13:

1 Timothy 6:6-8:

2. How does our culture discourage contentment?

3. How can you practice contentment?

Day four
Read Matthew 5:25-26 and Romans 13:1-7

1. Does the Lord require us to pay taxes to the government? Why?

Read James 2:1-9

2. What does Scripture say about partiality (showing favouritism)?

3. Are you ever guilty of partiality based on a person's financial, educational, colour or social status?

Read Romans 12:16 and Philippians 2:3

4. How do you plan to overcome partiality?

Day five
Read Acts 4:32-37 and 1 Thessalonians 4:11-12

1. What do these passages communicate to you about lifestyle?

   Acts 4:32-37:

   1 Thessalonians 4:11-12:

2. How do the following factors influence your present spending and lifestyle?

   Comparing your lifestyle with that of friends and other people:

Television, the Internet, magazines, catalogues, 'role models' and advertisements:

Your study of the Bible:

Your commitment to Christ and to things that are important to Him:

3. Do you sense that the Lord would have you change your spending or your standard of living? If so, in what way?

Day six
Read Deuteronomy 6:6-7; Proverbs 22:6 and Ephesians 6:4

1. According to these passages, who is responsible for teaching children how to handle money from a biblical perspective?

2. Stop and reflect for a few minutes: describe how well you were prepared to manage money when you first left home as a young person.

3. Describe how you currently or will train children to:

Budget – create and maintain a spending plan:

Work:

Give:

Save:

Spend wisely:

☐ **Please write your prayer requests in your prayer log before coming to the meeting.**

module six
Crown notes

To be read after completing **module six** personal study

This chapter explores God's perspective on a variety of issues: lifestyle, prosperity, taxes, and teaching children about money.

Lifestyle

The Bible does not require one standard of living for all. God places His people in every level of society — rich and poor — just as He did in the pages of Scripture. To help us evaluate our standard of living, we examine several principles that should influence our lifestyle.

1. Learn to be content

The apostle Paul wrote in 1 Timothy 6:8: *"if we have food and covering (clothes and shelter), with these we shall be content."* But our society operates on the assumptions that possessions equal happiness and more is always better. A modern advertisement would change Paul's message to read something like this, "If you can afford the finest food, wear the latest fashions, and live in a beautiful home, then you will be happy."

The majority of times the word 'contentment' appears in the Bible, it involves money. Paul wrote *"I have learned to be content whatever the circumstances. I know what it is to be in need, and I know what it is to have plenty. I have learned the secret of being content in any and every situation, whether well fed or hungry, whether living in plenty or in want. I can do everything through him who gives me strength"* (Philippians 4:11-13). Paul 'learned' to be content. He was not born with this instinct and neither are we; we must deliberately develop it.

The diagram below illustrates three components to the secret of contentment.

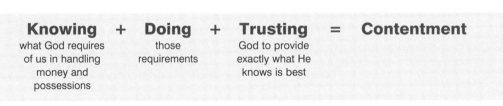

Knowing +	**Doing** +	**Trusting** =	**Contentment**
what God requires of us in handling money and possessions	those requirements	God to provide exactly what He knows is best	

Am I sacrificing a close relationship with Christ in the pursuit of wealth?

Merely knowing God's requirements is never enough to bring contentment; doing them is the key. We can trust our loving heavenly Father to provide exactly what He knows is best for us at any particular time — whether much or little. Biblical contentment has nothing to do with laziness or apathy. Because we serve the living and loving God, Christians should always seek to improve in all areas of their lives. Contentment does not exclude properly motivated ambition; instead, faithfully maximise the talents and possessions entrusted to you.

Biblical contentment is an inner peace that accepts what God has chosen for our present vocation and financial situation. *"Keep your life free from love of money and be content with what you have; for he has said, 'I will never fail you nor forsake you'"* (Hebrews 13:5, RSV).

2. Learn to avoid coveting

Coveting means craving another's property, and Scripture prohibits it. The last of the Ten Commandments is *"you shall not covet your neighbour's house. You shall not covet your neighbour's wife, or his manservant or maidservant, his ox or donkey, or anything that belongs to your neighbour"* (Exodus 20:17). Note the broad application: "anything that belongs to your neighbour." In other words, do not covet anything that belongs to anyone!

Greed, which is similar to coveting, is strongly condemned. *"But among you there must not be even a hint of sexual immorality, or of any kind of impurity, or of greed…For of this you can be sure that no immoral, impure or greedy person – such a man is an idolater – has any inheritance in the kingdom of Christ and of God"* (Ephesians 5:3, 5).

Greed and coveting have been called the silent sins. Rarely confronted, they are among the most common of sins. This is unfortunate, because they are a form of idolatry. When I began studying what the Bible teaches about money, I was overwhelmed by the extent of my own coveting. Ask God to show you if you are guilty of coveting something that is another's. If so, ask Him to change your heart.

3. Do not determine your lifestyle by comparing it to others

Some use comparison to justify spending more than they should. Many have suffered financially because they insisted on 'keeping up with the Joneses' even though they could not afford it. Someone once said "you can never keep up with the Joneses. Just when you thought you'd caught up, they go deeper in debt to buy more stuff!"

4. Freely enjoy whatever God allows you to purchase

Prayerfully submit spending decisions to God. Seeking His direction does not mean spending only for basic necessities.

A little while back, my wife asked me (repeatedly) to purchase a new dinner service. Well, what was wrong with the one we have, I thought? I promised to pray about it. As I prayed, God gave me peace about buying it, and now we continue to enjoy our new dinner service. *"Everything God created is good, and nothing is to be rejected if it is received with thanksgiving"* (1 Timothy 4:4).

5. Make an effort to live more simply

Every possession requires time, and often money, both to use and maintain. Too many, or the wrong types of possessions, can demand so much time or money that they harm our relationship with God and others. Most of the things you acquire demand your time to use, money to run or maintain and it may not be used as much as you anticipated. Look at what you have bought in the last twelve months and ask if you really needed to make that purchase. Often the answer will be 'yes,' but the success of online auctions bears evidence as to just how much is being bought and sold. A quiet, simple life is the safest environment for us to be able to invest enough time to nurture relationships.

"Make it your ambition to lead a quiet life, to mind your own business and to work with your hands, just as we told you, so that your daily life may win the respect of outsiders and so that you will not be dependent on anybody."

1 Thessalonians 4:11-12

Do not become unduly encumbered with the cares of this life. *"Endure hardship with us like a good soldier of Christ Jesus. No-one serving as a soldier gets involved in civilian affairs – he wants to please his commanding officer"* (2 Timothy 2:3-4).

6. Success is meaningless apart from serving Jesus Christ

King Solomon, the author of Ecclesiastes, had an annual income of more than £60 million. He lived in a palace that took 13 years to build. He owned 40,000 stalls of horses. His household's daily menu required 100 sheep and 30 oxen. Obviously, Solomon was in a position to know whether money could bring true happiness. He concluded *"Meaningless! Meaningless! Says the Teacher. Everything is meaningless!"* (Ecclesiastes 12:8). Nothing, even extraordinary success, can replace the value of our relationship with God. Ask yourself this question: am I sacrificing a close relationship with Christ in the pursuit of wealth? *"For what will it profit a man if he gains the whole world, and loses his own soul?"* (Mark 8:36, NKJV).

7. Do not be conformed to this world

Romans 12:2 says *"do not be conformed to this world."* The *Amplified® Bible* says it this way: *"Do not be conformed to this world (this age), fashioned after and adapted to its external, superficial customs."* We live in one of the most affluent cultures the world has ever known. Powerfully effective advertisements constantly tempt us to spend money by stressing the importance of image over function. For example, a car advertisement rarely focuses on its merits as reliable transportation; instead it projects an image of status or sex appeal.

No matter what the product – clothing, deodorants, credit cards or anything else – the message is clear; the happy, beautiful, wrinkle-free life can be ours if we are willing to buy it. Unfortunately, this has influenced all of us to some extent. One commentator put it this way, "People buy things they do not need with money they do not have to impress people they do not even like."

This graph depicts how the artificial, media-driven lifestyle influences our lives. The bottom curve represents our income – what we can afford to buy. The next curve illustrates what we actually spend. We make up the difference between our income and spending by the use of debt, which creates stress. The top of the graph demonstrates what advertisers tell us to buy – the expensive lifestyle that falsely claims to satisfy our deepest needs. When we want to live this unaffordable dream, we suffer discontentment.

From time to time we all get hooked on something we think we must buy. Once hooked, it is easy to rationalise any purchase. Remember to seek the Lord's guidance and godly counsel when making spending decisions.

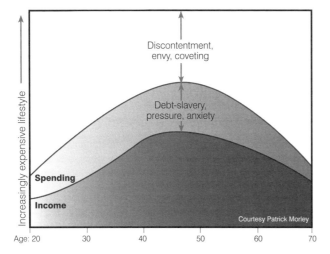

Artifical, media lifestyle

"Do not be conformed to this world"

Poverty, prosperity or stewardship?

Many Christians embrace one of two extreme financial philosophies. The first elevates poverty in the belief that a wealthy person cannot have a close relationship with Christ. However, not only does the Bible not say this, a number of godly people in it were among the wealthiest individuals of their day.

In the Old Testament, God extended the reward of abundance for obedience and the threat of poverty as a consequence of disobedience. *"I have set before you today life and good, death and evil, in that I command you today to love the Lord your God, to walk in His ways, and to keep His commandments, His statutes, and His judgements, that you may live and multiply; and the Lord your God will bless you"* (Deuteronomy 30:15-16).

Psalm 35:27 says *"the Lord…delights in the well-being of his servant."* We may pray for prosperity when our relationship with God is healthy and we have a proper perspective on possessions. *"Dear friend, I pray that you may enjoy good health and that all may go well with you, even as your soul is getting along well"* (3 John 2).

The other extreme, also an error, treats prosperity as the constant entitlement of all Christians who truly have faith. Study the life of Joseph, a faithful person who experienced both prosperity and poverty. Born into a prosperous family, his jealous brothers sold him into slavery. While a slave, Joseph's master promoted him to be head of his household. In that capacity, he was tempted but made the right choice not to commit adultery with his master's wife. That choice cost him many years in jail, but in God's timing, he was ultimately elevated to prime minister of Egypt and from that position was used to save his family.

The guideline for prosperity is found in Joshua 1:8 (KJV) *"this book of the law shall not depart out of thy mouth; but thou shalt meditate therein day and night, that thou mayest observe to do according to all that is written therein: for then thou shalt make thy way prosperous, and then thou shalt have good success."*

This passage offers two requirements for prosperity. Meditate on the Scriptures and do everything they command. When you do this, you place yourself in a position for God to entrust you with resources. There is no guarantee, however, that you will always prosper financially. Consider these four reasons of why the godly may not prosper:

1. Violating scriptural principles

Look again at Joshua 1:8. There is the requirement to do all that is written in the Bible. A person may be giving generously but acting dishonestly. A person may be honest but not fulfilling work responsibilities. A person may be a faithful employee but knee deep in debt. A person may be completely out of debt but not giving. One of the benefits of this study is that we explore what the entire Bible teaches about money. Those who do not understand all the requirements often neglect areas of responsibility unknowingly and suffer financially.

2. Building godly character

Many of the Bible's godly people lived righteously and yet lost their possessions. After slaying Goliath and becoming a national hero, David had to flee for his life from a tormented

King Saul. Job lost his children and possessions in the space of a few moments and was described as a *"blameless and upright, a man who fears God and shuns evil"* (Job 1:8). Paul learned the secret of contentment while suffering in prison even though he was righteous.

God sometimes moulds our character by allowing us to experience difficult circumstances. An example of how the Lord develops character in a people before prospering them is found in Deuteronomy 8:16-18: *"He gave you manna to eat in the desert, something your fathers had never known, to humble and to test you so that in the end it might go well with you. You may say to yourself, 'My power and the strength of my hands have produced this wealth for me.' But remember the Lord your God, for it is he who gives you the ability to produce wealth."* Our Father knows us better than we know ourselves. In His infinite wisdom, He knows exactly how much He can entrust to us at any time without it harming us.

3. Our dependence and His discipline

A father was carrying his two-year-old daughter as he waded in a lake. While they were close to shore, the child was unconcerned because of the apparent safety of the shore even though the water was deep enough to drown her. She didn't understand her dependence upon her father. The farther they moved away from shore, the tighter she held to her father. Like the child, we are always completely dependent upon God to provide for us even when we don't recognise it, because we are close to the shore of apparent financial security. But when our possessions are limited, it is easier to recognise our need and cling to Him.

And since even the godly sometimes stray, Hebrews 12:6, 10 tells us *"the Lord disciplines those he loves…for our good, that we may share in his holiness."* If we harbour unconfessed sin or a wrong attitude toward money, out of the Lord's great love for us He may discipline us by allowing financial difficulties to encourage us to forsake our sin.

4. The mystery of God's sovereignty

Hebrews 11 records "Faith's Hall of Fame." Verses 1-35 list people who triumphed miraculously by the exercise of their faith in God. Then in verse 36, the writer directs our attention to godly people who gained God's approval and yet experienced poverty. God ultimately chooses how much to entrust to each person, sometimes for reasons beyond our comprehension.

Lets summarise: The Scriptures teach neither the necessity of poverty nor uninterrupted prosperity/poverty. What the Bible teaches is the responsibility to be a faithful steward. Please review this chart contrasting the three perspectives.

	Poverty	Stewardship	Prosperity
Possessions are:	Evil	A responsibility	A right
I work to:	Meet only basic needs	Serve Christ	Become rich
Godly people are:	Poor	Faithful	Wealthy
Ungodly people are:	Wealthy	Unfaithful	Poor
I give:	Because I must	Because I love God	To get
My spending is:	Without gratitude to God	Prayerful and responsible	Carefree and all consuming

It is important to understand that God evaluates true riches based on His spiritual value system, which is stated most clearly in Revelation. The godly poor are rich in God's sight. *"I know your afflictions and your poverty – yet you are rich!"* (Revelation 2:9). Those who are wealthy without enjoying a close relationship with Christ are actually poor. *"You say, 'I am rich; I have acquired wealth and do not need a thing.' But you do not realise that you are wretched, pitiful, poor, blind and naked"* (Revelation 3:17). True prosperity extends far beyond material possessions. We can gauge it by how well we know Jesus Christ and how closely we follow Him.

Dangers of prosperity

Remember that God loves you deeply and wants to enjoy a close relationship with you. Because of His love, the Lord reveals dangers associated with money that can damage our relationship with Him and others.

First, wealth tends to separate people. Abram and Lot were relatives. Their prosperity ultimately caused them to move away from each other. *"Abram was very rich in livestock, in silver and in gold....(Lot) also had flocks and herds and tents. And the land could not sustain them while dwelling together, for their possessions were so great that they were not able to remain together"* (Genesis 13:2, 5-7, NASB). You probably know friends or family who have allowed conflicts over money to damage their relationships.

Second, it is easy for those who are prosperous to turn from God. *"When I have brought them into the land flowing with milk and honey, the land I promised on oath to their forefathers, and when they eat their fill and thrive, they will turn to other gods and worship them, rejecting me and breaking my covenant"* (Deuteronomy 31:20). After people become prosperous, they often take the Lord for granted, thinking they no longer need Him. Paul warned Timothy, *"command those who are rich in this present world not...to put their hope in wealth, which is so uncertain, but to put their hope in God"* (1 Timothy 6:17).

Third, it is difficult for the rich to come to know Jesus Christ as their Saviour. *"Jesus said to his disciples, 'I tell you the truth, it is hard for a rich man to enter the kingdom of heaven'"* (Matthew 19:23). Again, this is because the rich generally feel less of a need for God.

Fourth, riches can destroy a spiritually fruitful life. *"The one who received the seed that fell among the thorns is the man who hears the word, but the worries of this life and the deceitfulness of wealth choke it, making it unfruitful"* (Matthew 13:22). Riches are deceitful because they are tangible and can blind us from the reality of the unseen Lord. They seem capable of doing things that only Christ can really do.

Why do the wicked prosper?

This is a question God's people have asked for centuries. The prophet Jeremiah inquired of God: *"you are always righteous, O Lord, when I bring a case before you. Yet I would speak with you about your justice: Why does the way of the wicked prosper? Why do all the faithless live at ease?"* (Jeremiah 12:1).

The psalmist asked the same question when it seemed that godliness did not 'pay off.' Then the Lord revealed the wicked person's end – sudden eternal punishment:

Your questions

Q: How often should I review my Will?

A: Review it every three years – even sooner if you or your family experience significant changes or there is a change to the tax law.

"Surely God is good to…those who are pure in heart. But as for me…I envied the arrogant when I saw the prosperity of the wicked. When I tried to understand all this, it was oppressive to me till I entered the sanctuary of God; then I understood their final destiny. Surely you place them on slippery ground; you cast them down to ruin. How suddenly are they destroyed, completely swept away by terrors!"

Psalm 73:1-3, 16-19

The Bible tells us not to worry about or envy the wicked who prosper, because life on earth is short. *"Do not fret because of evil men or be envious of those who do wrong; for like the grass they will soon wither, like green plants they will soon die away"* (Psalm 37:1-2). We are to maintain God's perspective and His eternal value system.

Litigation

Hundreds of legal actions are filed each day in our country. Regrettably, some of these pit Christian against Christian. Suing seems to be developing into an increasing national pastime. Many factors contribute to this flood of legal action, including an avalanche of new laws; and, most disturbing, a growing tendency for people to be less and less forgiving. The court system uses an adversarial process, which frequently creates animosities between the parties involved. Instead of trying to heal, the system provides a legal solution but leaves the problems of unforgiveness and anger untouched.

The Bible stresses the goal of reconciliation. *"If you are offering your gift at the altar, and there remember that your brother has something against you, leave your gift there before the altar and go; first be reconciled to your brother"* (Matthew 5:23-24, RSV).

Scripture states that when Christians are at odds with one another, they should not settle their disputes through the courts. *"Dare any of you, having a matter against another, go to law before the unrighteous, and not before the saints? Do you not know that the saints will judge the world? And if the world will be judged by you, are you unworthy to judge the smallest matters? Do you not know that we shall judge angels? How much more, things that pertain to this life? If then you have judgements concerning things pertaining to this life, do you appoint those who are least esteemed by the church to judge? I say this to your shame. Is it so, that there is not a wise man among you, not even one, who will be able to judge between his brethren? But brother goes to law against brother, and that before unbelievers! Now therefore, it is already an utter failure for you that you go to law against one another. Why do you not rather accept wrong? Why do you not rather let yourselves be cheated?"* (1 Corinthians 6:1-7, NKJV).

Instead of initiating a legal action, there is a three-step procedure for Christians to resolve their differences set out in Matthew 18:15-17: *"if your brother sins against you, go and show him his fault, just between the two of you. If he listens to you, you have won your brother over. But if he will not listen, take one or two others along, so that 'every matter may be established by the testimony of two or three witnesses.' If he refuses to listen to them, tell it to the church; and if he refuses to listen even to the church, treat him as you would a pagan or a tax collector."*

1. **Go in private:** The person who believes he or she has been wronged needs to confront the other party in private with specific claims. If the dispute remains unresolved,

2. **Go with one or two others:** The person who feels wronged should return with witnesses who can confirm facts or help resolve the dispute. If this is unsuccessful,

3. **Go before the church:** The third step is mediation or arbitration before church leadership or a conciliation service.

The greatest benefit of following this procedure is not merely reaching a fair settlement of the dispute but practicing forgiveness and demonstrating love.

Taxes

What does God say about paying taxes? Someone asked Jesus that very question: *"'is it lawful for us to give tribute to Caesar or not?' But He recognised and understood their cunning and unscrupulousness and said to them, 'show Me a denarius (a coin)! Whose image and inscription does it have?' They answered, 'Caesar's.' He said to them, 'then render to Caesar the things that are Caesar's, and to God the things that are God's'"* (Luke 20:22-25, AMP). This is an example of the contrast between the practices of our society and the teaching of Scripture. Society says evade paying taxes. People rationalise, after all, the government seems to waste so much money.

But the Bible tells us to pay our taxes: *"everyone must submit himself to the governing authorities, for there is no authority except that which God has established. The authorities that exist have been established by God. This is also why you pay taxes, for the authorities are God's servants, who give their full time to governing. Give everyone what you owe him: If you owe taxes, pay taxes; if revenue, then revenue; if respect, then respect; if honour, then honour"* (Romans 13:1, 6-7). It is permissible to reduce taxes by using legal tax planning, but we should be careful not to make unwise decisions simply to avoid paying taxes or contemplate any form of tax evasion.

Partiality

Study this passage carefully: *"my brothers, as believers in our glorious Lord Jesus Christ, don't show favouritism. Suppose a man comes into your meeting wearing a gold ring and fine clothes, and a poor man in shabby clothes also comes in. If you show special attention to the man wearing fine clothes…have you not discriminated among yourselves and become judges with evil thoughts? If you really keep the royal law found in Scripture, 'love your neighbour as yourself,' you are doing right. But if you show favouritism, you sin and are convicted by the law as law-breakers"* (James 2:1-9).

I know many who have struggled with the sin of partiality and its unintentional influence on their actions. Once, when Howard hung up the phone, his wife said, "I know you were not talking to Ken; it must have been Ryan. You like Ken better, and it shows in your voice."

Partiality can be based on more than just a person's wealth. Other causes may be education, social position, colour or spiritual status. James 2:9 (NASB) could not be more blunt: *"If you show partiality, you are committing sin and are convicted by the law as transgressors."* How do we break the habit of partiality? Romans 12:10 tells us *"Be devoted to one another in brotherly love. Honour one another above yourselves."* And Philippians 2:3 reads *"in humility consider others better than yourselves."*

We need to ask God to help us develop the habit of elevating each person to be more important than ourselves. One practical way to overcome partiality is to concentrate on the abilities of each person. Focus on their positive attributes rather than the behavioural habits

One practical way to overcome partiality is to concentrate on the abilities of each person

that frustrate or annoy. Having managed over 200 staff I found I was initially on a steep learning curve. I started by finding people's faults and weaknesses and when this didn't work learnt to praise and appreciate them. Everyone can do some things better than I can. This realisation stops pride and helps me appreciate and accept all people.

Teaching children

In 1904, the country of Wales experienced a remarkable revival. The effects of the revival were widespread. An estimated 100,000 converts were added to the church during the two years the revival lasted, including previously hardened unbelievers. Drunkards, thieves, gamblers were transformed. Miners prayed together before commencing their shifts in the coal-mines. Pit-ponies, unused to the new kindness and clean language – without the usual kicks and curses – almost stopped work until they got adjusted. Courts had few cases to try. Whole football and rugby teams got converted and fixtures were abandoned. Dance halls were deserted, the pubs were empty and not a few went out of business, but the prayer meetings were crowded (from Great Revivals, Colin Whitaker). Wales also sent missionaries all over the world.

One of those missionaries travelled to the streets of Argentina, where he led a young boy to Christ. The boy's name was Luis Palau, now known as the 'Billy Graham of Latin America.' Many years later, Palau came to Wales to express his gratitude for being led to Christ. What he discovered was astonishing: less than one-half of one percent of the Welsh attended church. Divorce was at an all-time high and crime was increasing. The impact of Christianity had all but disappeared.

In response, Palau produced a film titled *God Has No Grandchildren*. The thrust of the film is that each generation is responsible for passing on the faith to the next.

Each generation is responsible for passing on the truths of Scripture, including God's financial principles, to its children. Proverbs 22:6 says *"train a child in the way he should go, and when he is old he will not turn from it."*

When you left home, how well prepared were you to make financial decisions? Parents and teachers spend years preparing young people for occupations but generally less than a few hours teaching children the value and use of the money they will earn during their careers.

Parents should be MVP parents. MVP is an acronym that describes the three methods to teach children God's way of handling money: Modelling, Verbal communication, and Practical opportunities. All three are needed to train your children. Let's look at each.

Modelling for our children

Since children soak up parental attitudes toward money like a sponge soaks up water, parents must model handling money wisely. Paul recognised the importance of modelling when he said *"follow my example, as I follow the example of Christ"* (1 Corinthians 11:1).

Luke 6:40 is a challenging passage. It reads *"everyone who is fully trained will be like his teacher."* Another way of saying this is that we can teach what we believe, but we only reproduce who we are. We must be good models.

Verbal communication

The Lord charged the Israelites *"these commandments that I give you today are to be upon your hearts. Impress them on your children. Talk about them when you sit at home and when you walk along the road, when you lie down and when you get up"* (Deuteronomy 6:6-7). We must verbally instruct children in the ways of the Lord, but children need more than verbal instruction; they also need a good example.

Practical experience

Children then need to be given opportunities to apply what they have heard and seen. There are learning experiences that benefit the child in the area of money management and money making.

Learning experiences in managing money

Learning to handle money should be part of a child's education. This is something parents must direct themselves and not delegate to teachers, because spending occurs outside the classroom. Consider five areas in which this is possible:

1. Income

As soon as children are ready for school, they should begin to receive pocket money to manage. Decide whether children should earn some, or all of the income, or receive it all as pocket money.

The amount will vary with the child's age, ability to earn, and the financial circumstances of the family. The amount is not as important as the responsibility of handling money. At first it is a new experience, and children will make many mistakes. Do not hesitate to let the 'law of natural consequences' run its course. You will be tempted to help when they immediately spend it all on an unwise purchase. But do not bail them out! Mistakes will be their best teacher.

Parents should establish boundaries and offer advice on how to spend, but children must have freedom of choice within those boundaries. The first few pennies and ten pences will make a lasting impression.

Every Saturday we would give our children their pocket money; Philip our eldest would often spend it, when out with his friends at the shops. Often his money would go on bubble gum in order to extend his collection of soccer cards. I am sure he learnt how to conduct surveys at school, he seemed to know how much pocket money everyone else was getting in the class and we were made to feel like a couple of meanies. But having built up a large pile of cards they were eventually consigned to his drawer, as he elected to budget his money so that it would last for the whole week.

2. Spending plan

When children begin receiving an income, teach them how to create and maintain a spending plan. Use a simple system, a three-compartment bank with each compartment labeled separately: GIVE, SAVE and SPEND. Children distribute a portion of their income into each compartment, creating a simple plan that uses visual control. Even a six-year-old can understand this method, because when the spending compartment is empty, he can't buy anything more!

You could use a shoe box and together make a money bank. Divide the box into three compartments, and on the outside label the compartments with the three categories. Then complete the money bank with three coin slots and remember to make sure the money cannot slide underneath from one compartment to another. If this happens the money may slide from saving to spending!

As children mature, they should participate in the family spending plan to help them understand the limitations of the family income. When they become teenagers, they should begin a written spending plan. If there is a computer at home encourage them to use a budgeting software program, alternatively use a notebook ruled with columns for analysing expenditure. Help them to become wise consumers by teaching shopping skills, the ability to distinguish needs from wants, and the importance of waiting on God to provide. Warn them about the powerful influence of advertising and the danger of impulse spending.

3. Saving and investing

Establish the habit of saving as soon as children receive an income. Begin by helping them open a savings account in their name. As they mature, discuss with them their options for saving. They may initially wish to use savings accounts that pay interest. If however they have enough money you may wish to introduce them to other types of investments such as ISAs and unit trusts. Teach them the benefits of compounding. If they grasp this concept and become faithful savers, they will enjoy financial stability as adults. Demonstrate this by saving for something that will directly benefit them. Using a graph they can fill in helps them visually chart the progress of saving.

Children should have both short-term and long-term saving goals. The younger the child, the more important short-term goals are. To four-year-olds, a week seems like a lifetime to save for a purchase. They will not understand saving for their future education but will get excited about saving for a small toy.

4. Debt

One way to teach children to avoid debt is to show them how difficult it is to get out of debt. A father loaned his son and daughter money to buy bicycles. He drew up a loan agreement that included the interest charged. After the children completed the long process of paying off the loan, the family celebrated with a 'loan burning' ceremony. The children appreciated those bikes more than any of their other possessions and vowed to avoid debt in the future.

5. Giving

Early childhood is the best time to establish the habit of giving. It is helpful for children to give a portion of their gifts to a tangible need they can see. For example, when their gift helps to refurbish, extend or acquire a new building or buy food for a needy family they know, they can understand its impact.

Richard Halverson, former U. S. Senate chaplain, gave his son, Chris, this heritage as a child. Chris gave money to support Kim, an orphan who had lost his sight during the Korean War, and thought of Kim as an adopted brother. One Christmas, Chris bought Kim

> **Help the children establish the habit of saving as soon as they receive an income**

a harmonica. Kim cherished this gift from Chris and learned to play it well. Today, Kim is an evangelist with a gospel presentation that includes playing the harmonica.

Teens benefit enormously by serving at a local homeless shelter or taking a mission trip to a country where there is deep poverty. This exposure can initiate a lifetime of giving to the poor. We also recommend a family time each week/month for dedicating that week/month's gifts to the Lord.

Learning experiences in managing money

Parents are also responsible for training children to develop proper work habits. Children who learn to enjoy work and are faithful at it will become productive and valuable in the job market where good employees can be difficult to find. There are three areas to consider in this training.

1. Learning routine responsibilities

The best way for young children to learn to work is to establish daily household chores for each member of the family.

2. Exposing your children to your work

Many children do not know how their fathers or mothers earn income. An important way to teach the value of work is to expose children to the parents' means of making a living.

One word of advice: because children are not usually with their parents at work, parents' work habits around the home will be a major influence. If a parent works hard away from home but complains about washing the dishes, what is being communicated to the children about work? Examine your work activities at home to ensure that you are properly influencing them.

3. Working for others

A paper round, baby-sitting job, shop assistant or waiter/waitressing job is an education. When children enter into an employee-employer relationship to earn extra money, they can learn the value of work and how to deal with others. Children who work with a good attitude are more satisfied and grow up with greater respect for the value of money and the effort required to earn it.

Prayer

One of the more valuable lessons you can teach children is to seek the Lord's guidance and provision through prayer. God wants to demonstrate that He is actively involved in our lives. One way He does this is by answering our prayers. We often rob ourselves of this opportunity by buying things or charging purchases onto 'plastic' without praying for God to meet the need.

One couple decided to ask their son to pray for some shirts he needed. After several months, a friend in the clothing business called to ask if their son needed shirts because he had excess stock in his size. They responded "absolutely!" and the friend brought 10 shirts to their home. That evening as their son began to pray for shirts, the father said "you don't need to pray for those anymore; God has answered that prayer." One by one they brought out the shirts. By shirt 10, their son thought God must be in the shirt business.

Single parents and grandparents

Single parents

Single parent families are increasingly common, and if you are one, I appreciate the added demands you face. Be encouraged – God defends the cause of single-parent families: *"He administers justice for the fatherless and the widow, and loves the stranger, giving him food and clothing"* (Deuteronomy 10:18, NKJV). And He sustains the fatherless: *"the Lord…sustains the fatherless and the widow"* (Psalm 146:9). My father left home when I was two and I lived in a single-parent family with my brother until I left home at the age of 20. Our home was poor and my clothes were usually bought from the 'nearly new shop.'

Some of the most faithful children are raised by single parents.

Grandparents

If you are a grandparent, you have a special opportunity to influence your grandchildren because of the unique role you can play. Unfortunately, many parents and grandparents have not agreed on how to train the next generation, leading to bruised relationships and ineffective training. Because grandparents can be very effective in complementing the objectives of parents, we recommend that they meet together to design a strategy for training their next generation to handle money.

When our first grandchild was born we immediately gave her parents a cheque for her child trust fund in the belief that one day this may assist with important costs such as education or her first home.

Strategy for independence

Finally, it is wise to establish a strategy for independence. Work towards having each child independently manage all of their own finances (with the exception of food and shelter) by the time they are 15. In this way you are available to advise the children as they learn to make spending decisions.

As Wales discovered, God has no grandchildren. Passing our faith in Christ to the next generation can be compared to a relay race. Any athletic coach will tell you that relay races can be won or lost in the passing of the baton from one runner to another. Runners rarely drop the baton once it is firmly in their grasp. If it is going to be dropped, it is in the exchange between the runners. Adults have the responsibility to pass the baton of practical biblical truths to the younger generation. This happens through training that sometimes shows little progress, but we urge you to be consistent and persistent! May our generation leave our children the blessed legacy of financial faithfulness.

module six
My notes

What I learnt from studying lifestyle:

What I plan to do differently:

My other notes:

module six
My notes

"Do not steal. Do not lie. Do not deceive one another"
(Leviticus 19:11)

module seven
Honesty

God's standard is absolute

module seven
Personal study

To be completed **prior to** module seven meeting

Scripture to memorise
"Do not steal. Do not lie. Do not deceive one another" (Leviticus 19:11)

Practical application
Implementation and fine tuning. Please review the month-by-month process for tracking your periodic expenses. You will also look at your month-end routines and how you will be able to reassess your spending budget.

Day one – let's review lifestyle
Read the lifestyle notes on pages 74-86 and answer:

1. What in the notes did you find of most help?

2. Do you sense the Lord would have you alter your lifestyle in anyway? If so, in what way?

Honesty

Day two
Read Leviticus 19:11-13; Deuteronomy 25:13-16; Ephesians 4:25 and 1 Peter 1:15-16

1. What do these verses communicate to you about God's demand for honesty?

   Leviticus 19:11-13:

Deuteronomy 25:13-16:

Ephesians 4:25:

1 Peter 1:15-16:

2. Are you consistently honest in even the smallest details? If not, what will you do to change?

3. What are two factors that motivate or influence us to act dishonestly?

4. How does this apply to you?

Day three
Read Exodus 18:21-22

1. Does the Lord require honesty for leaders? Why?

Read Proverbs 28:16 and Proverbs 29:12

2. What are the consequences of dishonesty for people in leadership?

Proverbs 28:16:

Proverbs 29:12:

3. How does this apply to you?

Day four
Read Proverbs 14:2

1. If you practice dishonesty, how does this affect our relationship with God?

Read Proverbs 26:28 and Romans 13:9-10

2. According to these passages, can you practice dishonesty and still love your neighbour? Why?

Day five
Read Psalm 15:1-5; Proverbs 12:22; Proverbs 20:7 and Isaiah 33:15-16

1. What are some of the benefits of honesty?

Psalm 15:1-5:

Proverbs 12:22:

Proverbs 20:7:

Isaiah 33:15-16:

Read Proverbs 3:32-33; Proverbs 13:11 and Proverbs 21:6

2. What are some of the curses of dishonesty?

Proverbs 3:32-33:

Proverbs 13:11:

Proverbs 21:6:

Day six
Read Exodus 22:1-4; Numbers 5:5-8 and Luke 19:8

1. What does the Bible say about restitution?

2. If you have acquired anything dishonestly, how will you make restitution?

Read Exodus 23:8; Proverbs 15:27 and Proverbs 29:4

3. What does Scripture say about bribes?

4. Have you ever been asked to give or take a bribe? If so, describe what happened.

☐ Please write your prayer requests in your prayer log before coming to the meeting.

module seven

Crown notes

To be read after completing **module seven** personal study

All of us have to make daily decisions about whether to handle money honestly. Do you tell the cashier at the shop when you receive too much change? Have you ever tried to sell something and been tempted not to tell the whole truth because you might lose the sale?

Honesty in society

These decisions are more difficult when so many around us are, at best economical with the truth, or at worse, are dishonest. After pumping £30 worth of petrol in my car, I asked for a receipt. When the attendant handed me a receipt for £50, I pointed out the mistake. His answer? "Oh, just record that in your books, and you'll get the cash out of your company and the tax relief. It's what everyone asks me to do."

When I heard that, my heart sank. The verse that came to mind was Judges 17:6: *"every man did what was right in his own eyes."* People today do the same thing, formulating their own standards of honesty and then changing them when circumstances change.

Honesty in Scripture

Hundreds of verses in the Bible communicate God's desire for us to be completely honest. For instance, Proverbs 20:23 says *"the Lord loathes all cheating and dishonesty"* (TLB). And Proverbs 12:22 states *"the Lord detests lying lips."* Study the following comparison between what the Scriptures teach and what our society practices concerning honesty.

Issue	Scripture	Society
Standard of honesty:	Complete honesty	Changes with circumstances
God's concern about honesty:	He requires it	There is no God or He looks the other way
The decision to be honest or dishonest is based upon:	Faith in the invisible, living God	Only the facts that can be seen
Question usually asked when deciding whether or not to be honest:	Will it please God?	Will I get away with it?

The God of truth

Truthfulness is one of God's attributes. He is repeatedly identified as the God of truth. *"I am…the truth"* (John 14:6). And He commands us to reflect His honest and holy character: *"but just as he who called you is holy, so be holy in all you do; for it is written: Be holy, because I am holy'"* (1 Peter 1:15-16).

In contrast to God's nature, John 8:44 describes the devil's character: *"he (the devil) was a murderer from the beginning, not holding to the truth, for there is no truth in him. When he lies, he speaks his native language, for he is a liar and the father of lies."* The Lord wants us to conform to His honest character rather than to the dishonest nature of the devil.

Absolute honesty

God wants us to be completely honest for the following reasons:

1. We cannot practice dishonesty and love God

Two of the Ten Commandments address honesty. *"You shall not steal. You shall not give false testimony against your neighbour"* (Exodus 20:15-16). And Jesus told us *"if you love me, you will obey what I command"* (John 14:15).

We cannot disobey by practicing dishonesty and still love God. When being dishonest, we behave as if the living God doesn't even exist! We believe that He is unable to provide exactly what we need even though He has promised to do so (Matthew 6:33). We take the situation into our own hands and do it our own dishonest way. We are also acting as if God is incapable of discovering our dishonesty and powerless to discipline us. If we really believe God will discipline us, we will not consider acting dishonestly.

Honest behaviour is an issue of faith. An honest decision may look foolish in light of what we can see, but the godly person knows Jesus Christ is alive even though invisible. Every honest decision strengthens our faith and helps us grow into a closer relationship with Christ. When we choose to be dishonest, we are denying our Lord. It is impossible to love God with all of our heart, soul, and mind if, at the same time, we are dishonest and act as if He does not exist. Scripture declares that the dishonest actually hate God. *"Those who follow the right path fear the Lord; those who take the wrong path despise him"* (Proverbs 14:2, NLT).

2. We cannot practice dishonesty and love our neighbour

God requires honesty because dishonest behaviour also violates the second commandment, *"love your neighbour as yourself"* (Mark 12:31). Romans 13:9-10 (TLB) reads *"if you love your neighbour as much as you love yourself you will not want to harm or cheat him, or kill him or steal from him….Love does no wrong to anyone."*

When we act dishonestly, we are stealing from another person. We may rationalise that it is a business or the government or an insurance company that is suffering loss. Yet, if we look at the bottom line, it is the business owners or fellow taxpayers or policy holders from whom we are stealing. It is just as if we took the money from their wallets. Dishonesty always injures people. The victim is always a person.

3. Credibility for evangelism

Honesty enables us to demonstrate the reality of Jesus Christ to those who do not yet know Him.

Are we as Christians good ambassadors for Christ? God has called us to be his witnesses and to spread the Gospel to our family, neighbours, in the workplace and beyond. Others will watch us and make judgements particularly as to whether being a Christian really makes a difference. Does your faith make a difference? Do you have something in your life that others want? When managing my businesses and employing those who were Christians I was acutely aware that the behaviour of those who were Christians was not always aligned with what others expected from those who professed to be Christians. We should be a lamp to those who do not know Christ – not a stumbling block.

Our actions speak louder than our words. *"Become blameless and pure, children of God without fault in a crooked and depraved generation, in which you shine like stars in the universe"* (Philippians 2:15).

Roger Downes, a home owner, had been planning an extension to his home for some time. Finally he and his wife contacted two builders for quotations. The first builder came round and after looking at the plans said his goodbye and told Roger that he would email a quote to him next week. The next builder also looked at the plans and asked Roger if anyone else was quoting. 'Yes,' said Roger. The builder checked what Roger did for a living (checking he did not work for HM Revenue & Customs) and then offered to do the extension at 20 percent less than any other quotation provided the job was cash so that no VAT would be charged.

Roger was tempted, but knew it would be wrong. He responded "I'm sorry, I can't do that because I am a Christian and I cannot be involved in something that is dishonest."

"You should have seen the look on the builder's face, he almost went into shock," Roger said. Then an interesting thing happened. The builder returned three days later to apologise for what he had said and asked Roger what was so important to him when he could have saved thousands of pounds. That was Roger's chance to share his faith and invite the builder to church.

Honest behaviour confirms to those who do not yet know Him that we serve a holy God.

4. Confirms God's direction

Proverbs 4:24-26 reads *"put away perversity from your mouth; keep corrupt talk far from your lips. Let your eyes look straight ahead, fix your gaze directly before you. Make level paths for your feet and take only ways that are firm."* Choosing to walk the narrow path of honesty eliminates the many possible avenues of dishonesty.

"If only I'd understood that," Dan said. "Lucy and I wanted that house so much. It was our dream home. But we had too much debt to qualify for the mortgage. The only way for us to buy it was to hide some of our debts from the bank.

"It was the worst decision of our lives. Almost immediately we were unable to meet the mortgage payment and pay our other debts too. The pressure built and was more than Lucy could stand. Our dream house ended up being a family nightmare. I not only lost the house but nearly lost my wife."

Had Dan and Lucy been honest, the bank would not have approved the loan, and they would have been unable to purchase that particular home. Had they prayed and waited, God might have brought something more affordable, thus avoiding the pressure that almost ended their marriage. Honesty helps confirm God's direction.

Your questions

Q: Is is permissible to reduce my taxes by using legal tax planning?

A: Yes, Absolutely! You should use tax planning and pay whatever is due. It is okay to avoid a tax liability but not to evade it.

5. Even small acts of dishonesty are harmful

God requires us to be absolutely honest because even the smallest act of dishonesty is sin and interrupts our fellowship with God. The smallest 'white lie' hardens our hearts, making our consciences increasingly insensitive to sin and deafening our ears to God's voice. This single cancer cell of small dishonesty multiplies and spreads to greater dishonesty. *"He who is dishonest in a very little is dishonest also in much"* (Luke 16:10, RSV).

An event in Abraham's life challenges us to be honest in small matters. The king of Sodom offered him all the goods he had recovered when he had rescued the people of Sodom. But Abraham responded *"I have raised my hand to the Lord, God Most High, Creator of heaven and earth, and have taken an oath that I will accept nothing belonging to you, not even a thread or the thong of a sandal"* (Genesis 14:22-23).

Just as Abraham was unwilling to take so much as a thread, we challenge you to make a similar commitment. Decide not to make a false benefit claim, browse the Internet or answer emails when you should be working, take goods or materials or steal a long distance phone call from your employer, the government or anyone else. The people of God must be honest in even the smallest matters.

To love God and our neighbours, to evangelise effectively, to confirm God's direction and to develop a heart sensitive to God – is there any wonder that our Lord knows it is best for us to be completely honest?

6. Workplace honesty as an employer

In business? Always deal with employees honestly, particularly with regard to their performance and their employment. Ensure no personal costs are processed through the business accounts and that your costs for tax relief are wholly and exclusively incurred in the course of your business!

Escaping the temptation of dishonesty

A teacher was teaching these principles in a secular school when a young man raised his hand and said "I think we all would like to be the person you're talking about, but I know that if the right opportunity comes along, I'm going to be dishonest." I think he is correct. Apart from living our lives yielded to the Holy Spirit, all of us will be dishonest.

"Live by the Spirit, and you will not gratify the desires of the sinful nature. For the sinful nature desires what is contrary to the Spirit, and the Spirit what is contrary to the sinful nature."
Galatians 5:16-17

"Live by the spirit, and you will not gratify the desires of the sinful nature"

The character of our human nature is to act dishonestly. *"Out of men's hearts, come evil thoughts…theft…deceit"* (Mark 7:21-22). The desire of the Spirit is for us to be honest. The absolutely honest life is supernatural. We need to submit ourselves entirely to Jesus Christ as Lord and allow Him to live His life through us. There is no other way.

1. The Golden Rule

"Let each of you look out not only for his own interests, but also for the interests of others." (Philippians 2:4, NKJV). This verse is better translated, 'look intently' after the interests of others. God used this passage to point out John's lack of concern for others just when he was about to purchase some land, taking advantage of a seller who knew nothing of

its value. John secretly congratulated himself because he knew the purchase price he had offered was very low. Not once had he considered what would be fair to the seller. He had concentrated solely on acquiring the property at the lowest possible price.

John reexamined the transaction in the light of 'looking intently' after the seller's interests as well as his own. After an intense inner struggle, he concluded that he should pay more for the property to reflect its true value. Practicing the Golden Rule is sometimes costly, but its reward is a clear conscience before God and other people.

> **"Do unto others as you would have them do unto you"**

2. Maintain a healthy fear of the Lord

When we talk of a 'healthy fear' of the Lord, we are not implying that God is a big bully just waiting for the opportunity to punish us. Rather, He is a loving Father who, out of infinite love, disciplines His children for their benefit. *"God disciplines us for our good, that we may share in his holiness"* (Hebrews 12:10).

One of the methods God uses to motivate honesty in us is this 'healthy fear.' Proverbs 16:6 says *"through the fear of the Lord a man avoids evil."* Hebrews 12:11 warns us: *"no discipline seems pleasant at the time, but painful."* Discipline hurts! Given the choice, we should obey His Word rather than make a deliberate decision that will prompt our loving Father to discipline us.

We believe our heavenly Father will not allow us to keep anything we have acquired dishonestly. Proverbs 13:11 reads *"dishonest money dwindles away."*

A friend purchased four azalea plants, but the sales counter had only charged her for one. She knew it, but she left the garden centre without paying for the other three. She said it was miraculous how quickly three of those plants died!

Think about this for a moment: if you are a parent and one of your children steals something, do you allow the child to keep it? Of course not, because keeping it would damage the child's character. Not only do you insist on its return, but you usually want the child to experience enough discomfort to produce a lasting impression. For instance, you might have the child confess the theft to the sales cashier. When our heavenly Father lovingly disciplines us, He usually does it in a way we will not forget.

3. Stay away from dishonest people

Scripture teaches that we are deeply influenced by those around us, either for good or for evil. David recognised this and said *"my eyes will be on the faithful in the land, that they may dwell with me; he whose walk is blameless will minister to me. No-one who practises deceit will dwell in my house; no-one who speaks falsely will stand in my presence"* (Psalm 101:6-7). Paul wrote *"do not be misled: Bad company corrupts good character"* (1 Corinthians 15:33). Solomon was even stronger: *"the accomplice of a thief is his own enemy"* (Proverbs 29:24).

Obviously, we cannot isolate ourselves from every dishonest person. In fact, we are to be 'salt and light' in the world (Matthew 5:13-16). We should, however, be very cautious when choosing our close friends or considering a business relationship with another.

If I observe a person who is dishonest in dealing with the government or in a small matter, I know this person will be dishonest in greater matters and probably in dealing with me. In our opinion, it is impossible for people to be selectively honest. Either they have made the commitment to be completely honest or their dishonesty will become more prevalent. It is much easier to remain absolutely honest if you are surrounded by others with the same conviction.

4. Give generously

We can help escape the temptation of acting dishonestly by giving generously to those in need. *"Let him that stole steal no more: but rather let him labour, working with his hands the thing which is good, that he may have to give to him that needeth"* (Ephesians 4:28, KJV).

What to do when we have been dishonest

Unfortunately, we sometimes slip and act dishonestly. Once we recognise it, we need to do the following.

1. Restore our fellowship with God

Anytime we sin, we break fellowship with God and need to restore it. 1 John 1:9 (KJV) tells us how: *"if we confess our sins, he is faithful and just to forgive us our sins, and to cleanse us from all unrighteousness."* We must agree with God that our dishonesty was sin and then thankfully accept His gracious forgiveness so we can again enjoy His fellowship. Remember, God loves us. He is kind and merciful. God is ready to forgive our dishonesty when we turn from it.

2. Restore our fellowship with the harmed person

After our fellowship with God has been restored, we need to confess our dishonesty to the person we offended. *"Confess your sins to one another"* (James 5:16).

A handful of people have confessed wronging me. Interestingly, these people have become some of my closest friends – in part because of my respect for them. They so desired an honest relationship that they were willing to expose their wrongdoings.

Confessing is not normally easy. In fact, it's hard. Several years ago I went to someone I had wronged and confessed my sin. It had taken me some years to take the step; however my pride had stood in the way. Afterwards I sensed a great freedom in our relationship; I also discovered that, because it is a painfully humbling experience, confession helps break the habit of dishonesty. Today, that person lives in London over 100 miles from Bristol, he is one of my counsellors and we enjoy a close friendship whereby we are both able to help one another.

Failing to confess and restore fellowship may result in a lack of financial prosperity. *"He who conceals his transgressions will not prosper, but he who confesses and forsakes them will obtain mercy"* (Proverbs 28:13, RSV).

3. Restore dishonestly acquired property

If we have acquired anything dishonestly, we must return it to its rightful owner. *"Then it shall be, when he sins and becomes guilty, that he shall restore what he took by robbery…or anything about which he swore falsely; he shall make restitution for it in full and add to it one-fifth more. He shall give it to the one to whom it belongs"* (Leviticus 6:4-5, NASB).

Restitution is a tangible expression of repentance and an effort to correct a wrong. Zacchaeus is a good example. He promised Jesus *"if I have cheated anybody out of anything, I will pay back four times the amount"* (Luke 19:8).

If it's not possible for restitution to be made, then the property should be given to God. Numbers 5:8 teaches *"if that person has no close relative to whom restitution can be made for the wrong, the restitution belongs to the Lord and must be given to the priest, along with the ram with which atonement is made for him."*

> **Restitution is a tangible expression of repentance**

Honesty required for leaders

God is especially concerned with the honesty of leaders.

Influence of leaders

Leaders influence those who follow them. The owner of a haulage company began wearing trainers to work. Within six months, all the men in his office were in trainers. He suddenly changed to traditional business shoes, and six months later all the men were wearing business shoes.

In a similar way, a dishonest leader produces dishonest followers. *"If a ruler listens to lies, all his officials become wicked"* (Proverbs 29:12). Leaders of a business, church, or home must set the example of honesty in their personal lives before those under their authority can be expected to do the same.

The president of a large international construction company was asked why her company did not work in countries where bribes were common. She responded "we never build in those countries because we can't afford to. If my employees know we are acting dishonestly, they will eventually become thieves. Their dishonesty will ultimately cost us more than we could ever earn on a project."

During an effort to reduce expenses, a company discovered the employees were making frequent personal long-distance telephone calls at the office and charging them to the company. The managing director had unwittingly fueled this problem. He had reasoned that because he placed approximately the same number of company long-distance calls on his home phone as personal long-distance calls on the company phone, detailed accounting was unnecessary. His employees, however, knew only of his calls at work. They concluded that if this practice was acceptable for the boss, it was acceptable for all. Leaders should *"abstain from all appearance of evil"* (1 Thessalonians 5:22, KJV) because their actions influence others.

Selection of leaders

Dishonesty should disqualify a person from leadership. Listen to the counsel of Jethro, Moses' father-in-law. *"Select capable men from all the people, men who fear God, trustworthy men who hate dishonest gain, and appoint them as officials over thousands, hundreds, fifties and tens"* (Exodus 18:21).

Two of the four criteria for leadership selection dealt with honesty: "men of truth, those who hate dishonest gain." We believe God wants us to continue to select leaders based on these same character qualities.

Preservation of leaders

Not only are leaders selected in part by honest behaviour, but a leader retains this position by acting honestly. *"A ruler…who hates corruption will have a long life"* (Proverbs 28:16). We have all witnessed leaders in business or government who have been removed because of personal corruption.

How can a leader maintain the standard of absolute honesty? By becoming accountable to others. It is necessary to establish a system of checks and balances that do not usurp the leader's authority but provide a structure to ensure accountability.

Bribes

A bribe is defined as anything given to influence a person to do something illegal or wrong. The taking of bribes is clearly prohibited in Scripture: *"do not accept a bribe, for a bribe blinds those who see and twists the words of the righteous"* (Exodus 23:8). Bribes frequently come packaged as 'gifts' or 'referral fees.' Evaluate any such offer to confirm that it is not a bribe in disguise.

Blessings and curses

Listed below are some of the blessings God has promised for the honest and some of the curses reserved for the dishonest. Read these slowly and prayerfully, asking God to use His Word to motivate you to a life of honesty.

Blessings for the honest:
- Blessing of a more intimate relationship with the Lord: *"for the Lord detests a perverse man but takes the upright into His confidence"* (Proverbs 3:32).
- Blessings on the family: *"the righteous man leads a blameless life; blessed are his children after him"* (Proverbs 20:7).
- Blessings of life: *"truthful lips endure for ever, but a lying tongue lasts only a moment"* (Proverbs 12:19).
- Blessings of prosperity: *"the house of the righteous contains great treasure, but the income of the wicked brings them trouble"* (Proverbs 15:6).

Curses reserved for the dishonest:
- Curse of alienation from God: *"for the Lord detests a perverse man"* (Proverbs 3:32).
- Curse on the family: *"a greedy man brings trouble to his family, but he who hates bribes will live"* (Proverbs 15:27).
- Curse of death: *"fortune made by a lying tongue is a fleeting vapor and a deadly snare"* (Proverbs 21:6).
- Curse of poverty: *"dishonest money dwindles away"* (Proverbs 13:11).

Did you know?

Shoplifting costs more than £200 million a year, a cost which is increasing. Shoplifters stole on average more than £150 worth of goods at a time.

module seven
My notes

What I learnt from studying honesty:

What I plan to do differently:

My other notes:

"Remember the words of the Lord Jesus, that He Himself said, 'It is more blessed to give than to receive'"
(Acts 20:35, NKJV)

module eight
Giving

Giving is blessed

module eight
Personal study

To be completed **prior to** module eight meeting

Scripture to memorise
"Remember the words of the Lord Jesus, that He Himself said, 'It is more blessed to give than to receive'" (Acts 20:35, NKJV)

Practical application
Having completed the budgeting and spending plan you will look this week at organising your estate and your Will.

Day one – let's review honesty
Read the honesty notes on pages 94-101 and answer:

1. How does the example of Abraham (Abram) in Genesis 14:21-23 challenge you to be honest?

2. Ask God to reveal any areas of dishonesty in your life. How do you propose to deal with these areas?

Giving

Day two
Read Micah 6:6-8; Matthew 23:23;1 Corinthians 13:3 and 2 Corinthians 9:7

1. What do each of these passages communicate about the actions we should adopt when giving?

Micah 6:6-8:

Matthew 23:23

1 Corinthians 13:3:

2 Corinthians 9:7:

2. How can a person develop a proper attitude in giving?

3. How would you describe your attitude in giving?

Day three
Read Acts 20:35

1. How does this principle from God's economy differ from the way most people view giving?

Read Proverbs 11:24-25; Matthew 6:20; Luke 12:34 and 1 Timothy 6:18-19

2. List the benefits for the giver that are found in each of the following passages:

Proverbs 11:24-25:

Matthew 6:20:

Luke 12:34:

1 Timothy 6:18-19:

Day four
Read Malachi 3:8-10

1. How did God view the failure to tithe (give 10 percent)?

Read 2 Corinthians 8:1-5

2. Identify three principles from this passage that should influence how much you give.

Prayerfully (with your spouse if you are married) seek the Lord's guidance to determine how much you should give. You will not be asked to disclose the amount.

Day five
Read Numbers 18:8-10, 24; Galatians 6:6 and 1 Timothy 5:17-18

1. What do these verses tell you about financially supporting your church and those who teach the Scriptures?

    Numbers 18:8-10, 24:

    Galatians 6:6:

    1 Timothy 5:17-18:

Day six
Read Ezekiel 16:49; Isaiah 58:6-11 and Luke 4:17-18

1. What do these verses say about what we should give to the poor?

   Ezekiel 16:49:

   Isaiah 58:6-11:

   Luke 4:17-18:

Read Matthew 25:35-46

2. How does Jesus Christ identify with the needy?

Read Galatians 2:9-10

3. What does this verse communicate to you about giving to the poor?

4. Are you currently giving to the needy? Should your giving change?

☐ Please write your prayer requests in your prayer log before coming to the meeting.

module eight
Crown notes

To be read after completing **module eight** personal study

Few areas of the Christian life can be more misunderstood and frustrating than that of giving. For several years after I accepted Christ, I did my best to avoid giving. On those occasions when I felt obligated to give in order to appear spiritual, I did so, but my heart wasn't in it.

For many years after I accepted Christ, even until after I was married, I understood little of the importance of giving. While living in Atlanta I purchased a copy of the USA Today newspaper. Every day they include a 'snapshot' survey; one day the survey asked of those earning $50,000 'how much do you need to be comfortable?' The average answer was $75,000. The same question was asked of those who earned $100,000 – their answer – $250,000. In Haggai 1:6 God reveals: *"You eat, but never have enough. You drink, but never have your fill. You put on warm clothes, but are not warm. You earn wages, only to put them in a purse with holes in it."* When is enough enough? The love of money is never satisfied. In Ecclesiastes 5:12b we read *"but the abundance of the rich will not permit him to sleep."* Isn't that evidenced by the snapshot? There are those who never have enough. The more they have, the more they want. God's way of breaking the cycle of greed is to give.

How easy is it? My response to that is 'it's not!' To me giving just doesn't come as naturally as it should, but by the Spirit of God I am a new creation and know that the Bible is replete with warnings against loving money. Being able to give joyfully as He leads has been an amazing experience and a source of great joy knowing that I can invest as He leads me in what He is doing.

Intense competition for resources makes these decisions even more difficult. It seems as if we are always hearing about and receiving requests for support. I have even received a request for support by text message.

I react to these requests with mixed emotions: compassion, gratitude, guilt and even cynicism. I feel deep compassion and almost despair when confronted with those facing starvation of body or spirit. I am grateful for the people whose life purpose is to meet those needs. I feel guilty that perhaps we are not giving enough. Sometimes I feel cynical about being solicited and perhaps manipulated by people whose goals may be worthwhile but whose methods are questionable.

We will examine four elements of giving: attitudes, advantages, amount and approach.

Above all else, giving directs our heart to Christ

Attitudes in giving

God evaluates our actions on the basis of our attitudes. John 3:16 reveals His attitude toward giving: *"for God so loved the world that he gave his one and only Son."* Note the sequence. Because God loved, He gave. Because God is love, He is also a giver. He set the example of giving motivated by love.

An attitude of love in giving is crucial: *"if I give all I possess to the poor...but have not love, I gain nothing"* (1 Corinthians 13:3). What could be more commendable than giving everything to the poor? However, giving without an attitude of love provides no benefit to the giver.

In God's economy, the attitude is more important than the amount. Jesus emphasised this in Matthew 23:23: *"woe to you, teachers of the law and Pharisees, you hypocrites! You give a tenth of your spices – mint, dill and cummin. But you have neglected the more important matters of the law – justice, mercy and faithfulness. You should have practised the latter, without neglecting the former."* The Pharisees had been careful to give the correct amount, but Christ rebuked them because of their attitude. He looks past the amount of the gift to the heart of the giver.

We can consistently give with love when we recognise that we are giving to God Himself. We see an example of this in Numbers 18:24: (NASB) *"The tithe of the sons of Israel...they offer as an offering to the Lord."* If giving is merely to a church, a ministry, or a needy person, it is only charity. But giving to God is always an act of worship, expressing love and gratitude to our Creator, our Saviour and our faithful Provider. Whenever we put something in the offering plate, we should remind ourselves that our gift goes to God Himself.

In addition to giving with love, we are to give cheerfully. *"Each man should give what he has decided in his heart to give, not reluctantly or under compulsion, for God loves a cheerful giver"* (2 Corinthians 9:7). The original Greek word for cheerful is *hilarios*, which is translated into the English word *hilarious*. We are to be joyful givers.

When was the last time you saw hilarity when the offering plate passed? The atmosphere more often reminds us of a patient in the dentist chair awaiting a painful extraction. So, how do we develop this hilarity in our giving? Consider the early churches of Macedonia: *"we want you to know about the grace that God has given the Macedonian churches. Out of the most severe trial, their overflowing joy and their extreme poverty welled up in rich generosity"* (2 Corinthians 8:1-2).

How did the Macedonians, who were in terrible circumstances, 'severe trial' and 'extreme poverty,' still manage to give with 'overflowing joy?' The answer is in verse five: *"they gave themselves first to the Lord and then to us in keeping with God's will."* The key to cheerful giving is to yield ourselves to Christ and ask Him to direct how much He wants us to give. That places us in a position to experience the advantages of giving with the proper attitude.

Stop and examine yourself. What is your attitude toward giving?

Advantages of giving

Gifts obviously benefit the recipient. The church continues its ministry, the hungry are fed, the naked are clothed and missionaries are sent. But in God's economy, gifts given with the proper attitude also benefit the giver. *"Remembering the words of the Lord Jesus, how he said, 'It is more blessed to give than to receive'"* (Acts 20:35, RSV). As we examine Scripture, we find that the giver benefits in four areas.

1. Increase in intimacy with Christ

Above all else, giving directs our hearts to Christ. Matthew 6:21 tells us *"for where your treasure is, there your heart will be also."* This is why it is necessary to give each gift to the person of Jesus Christ: it draws our heart to Him.

Look again at the faithful steward in the parable of the talents? His reward – *"come and share your master's happiness"* (Matthew 25:21). Giving is one of your responsibilities as a steward; and the more faithful you are in fulfilling your responsibilities, the more you can enter into the joy of knowing Christ intimately. Nothing in life compares with that.

2. Development of character

Our heavenly Father wants us – His children – to conform to the image of His Son. The character of Christ is that of an unselfish giver. Unfortunately, humans are selfish by nature. One essential way we become conformed to Christ is by regular giving. Someone once said "giving is not God's way of raising money; it is God's way of raising people into the likeness of His Son."

3. Treasures in heaven

Matthew 6:20 reads *"store up for yourselves treasures in heaven, where moth and rust do not destroy, and where thieves do not break in and steal."* God tells us that heaven has its own 'Royal Bank of Heaven,' where we can invest for eternity.

Paul wrote *"not that I am looking for a gift, but I am looking for what may be credited to your account"* (Philippians 4:17). Each of us has an account in heaven that we will be able to enjoy for eternity. And although it is true that we 'can't take it with us when we die,' Scripture teaches that we can make deposits to our heavenly account before we die.

4. Increase on earth

Many people have a hard time believing that giving results in blessings flowing back to the giver; however, study the following passages:

Proverbs 11:24-25 says *"one man gives freely, yet gains even more; another withholds unduly, but comes to poverty. A generous man will prosper; he who refreshes others will himself be refreshed ."*

Examine 2 Corinthians 9:6-11: *"whoever sows sparingly will also reap sparingly, and whoever sows generously will also reap generously…God is able to make all grace abound to you, so that in all things at all times, having all that you need, you will abound in every good work.…Now He who supplies seed to the sower and bread for food will also supply and increase your store of seed and will enlarge the harvest of your righteousness. You will be made rich in every way so that you can be generous on every occasion, and through us your generosity will result in thanksgiving to God."*

These verses clearly teach that giving results in an increase: *"will also reap bountifully…always having all sufficiency in everything…may have an abundance…will supply and multiply your seed…you will be enriched in everything."*

Is this a source reference point for those that proclaim the prosperity gospel? We should accept that God does want His children to prosper, not in finances alone but in body, mind and spirit. However, some of the most precious gifts that God gives are those that money can't buy and death can't steal.

But note carefully why God returns a material increase: *"Always having all sufficiency in everything, you may have an abundance for every good deed…will supply and multiply your seed for sowing…you will be enriched in everything for all liberality."* As shown in the diagram below, the Lord produces an increase so that we may give more and have our needs met at the same time.

If you close your hand you keep what is in your hand from getting out and as a consequence you cannot give or maybe you give with a mean spirit. We live in a unique time when there is vast wealth being handed down from the baby boomer generation. What if that wealth were to be partly invested in the Kingdom of God? What eternal dividends would that investment yield? It does, after all, belong to God. Interestingly, the hand that is closed cannot receive either.

Study the cycle of giving

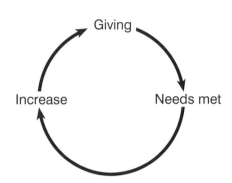

One reason God reveals that we can anticipate increase is because He wants us to recognise that He is behind it. God has chosen to be invisible, but He wants us to experience His reality.

When we give we should not do so out of a motive of seeking a return, for God wants us to give willingly and not out of a 'give and get' mentality. God can be very creative! Remember, givers experience the advantages of giving, only when they give cheerfully and with love – not when the motive is just to get.

Amount to give

Let's look at what the Bible says about how much to give. Before the Old Testament Law, there were two instances of giving a known amount. In Genesis 14:20, Abraham (Abram) gave 10 percent – a tithe – after the rescue of his nephew Lot. And in Genesis 28:22, Jacob promised to give God a tenth of all his possessions if God brought him safely through his journey.

With the Law came the requirement of the tithe. The Lord condemns the children of Israel in Malachi 3:8-9 for not tithing properly: *"will a man rob God? Yet you rob me. But you ask, 'How do we rob you?' In tithes and offerings. You are under a curse – the whole nation of you – because you are robbing me!'"*

In addition to the tithe, there were various offerings. God also made special provision for the poor. Every seven years all debts were cancelled; every 50 years the land was returned to the original land-owning families. Special harvesting rules allowed the poor to glean behind the harvesters.

God made another significant provision for the poor in Deuteronomy 15:7-8: (RSV) *"if there is among you a poor man, one of your brethren, in any of your towns within your land which the Lord your God gives you, you shall not harden your heart or shut your hand against your poor brother, but you shall open your hand to him, and lend him sufficient for his need, whatever it may be."* Even under the law, the extent of one's giving was not to be limited by a fixed percentage but was to be adjusted by surrounding needs.

The New Testament teaches that we are to give in proportion to the material blessing we receive. It also commends sacrificial giving. What I like about the tithe is that it is systematic, and the amount of the gift is easy to compute. The danger of the tithe is that it can be treated as simply another bill to be paid; this attitude does not place us in a position to receive the blessings God has for us when we give. Another potential danger of tithing is the assumption that once we have tithed we have fulfilled all of our obligations to give. For many Christians, the tithe should be the beginning of their giving, not the limit.

How much should you give? To answer this question, first give yourself to God. Submit yourself to Him. Earnestly seek His will for you concerning giving. Ask Him to help you obey Christ's leading. We are convinced that we should tithe as a minimum and then give over and above the tithe as God prospers or directs us.

Approach to giving

During Paul's third missionary journey, one of his priorities was to take up a collection for the suffering believers in Jerusalem. We draw several practical applications from his instructions concerning this collection. *"On the first day of every week, each one of you should set aside a sum of money in keeping with his income, saving it up, so that when I come no collections will have to be made"* (1 Corinthians 16:2). Even when finances are stretched, always give or you may never have enough to give. The underlying principle of generosity is that stinginess leads to poverty while it is the one who gives who receives.

For those who like alliteration our seven P's of giving are:

1. Giving should be periodic
"On the first day of every week." God understands that we need to give frequently. Giving only once a year is a mistake. We need to give regularly to be drawn consistently to Christ.

2. Giving should be personal
"Each one of you is to give." It is the responsibility of every child of God, whether young or old, rich or poor, to give. The advantages of giving are intended for each person, and each one must participate to enjoy them.

3. Giving should be out of a private deposit
"Put aside and save." If you experience difficulty in monitoring the money you have decided to give, consider opening a separate account or setting aside a special 'giving jar' into which you deposit the money you intend to give. Then, as needs are brought to your attention, the money is ready to meet those needs.

4. Giving should be a priority
"Honour the Lord with your wealth, with the firstfruits of all your crops" (Proverbs 3:9). As soon as we receive any income, we should set aside the amount we are going to give. This habit helps us to put Christ first in all we do and defeats the temptation to spend what we have decided to give.

Do not wait for leaders, do it alone, person to person

Mother Teresa

5. Giving should be proportionate

"Each one of you should set aside a sum of money in keeping with his income" (1 Corinthians 16:2). The Old Testament tithe was proportionate, not fixed. If someone earned 200 pieces of gold the tithe was 20 pieces, if another earned 100 pieces the tithe was 10 pieces. Proportionate giving is not equal giving and involves greater sacrifice for those on lower incomes, although it is often those with larger incomes who give less proportionately.

6. Giving should be premeditated

"Every man according as he purposed in his heart" (2 Corinthians 9:7, KJV). We should give prayerfully, exercising the same care in selecting where we give as we do when deciding where to invest.

7. Giving should be without pride

To experience any of God's benefits, do not give to impress people.

"Be careful not to do your 'acts of righteousness' before men, to be seen by them. If you do, you will have no reward from your Father in heaven. So when you give to the needy, do not announce it with trumpets, as the hypocrites do in the synagogues and on the streets, to be honoured by men…they have received their reward in full. But when you give to the needy, do not let your left hand know what your right hand is doing, so that your giving may be in secret. Then your Father, who sees what is done in secret, will reward you."

Matthew 6:1-4

Places for giving

In the Bible we are instructed to give to three areas: the local church, ministries, and the poor and needy.

> **Jesus, the Creator of all things, personally identifies Himself with the poor**

1. Giving to the local church and Christian ministries

Throughout its pages, the Bible focuses on funding the ministry. The Old Testament priesthood received specific support: *"I give to the Levites all the tithes in Israel…in return for the work they do while serving at the Tent of Meeting"* (Numbers 18:21) and New Testament teaching on ministerial support is just as strong. Unfortunately, some have wrongly taught poverty for Christian workers, influencing many to believe that everyone in Christian ministry should be poor. That position is not scriptural.

"Pastors who do their work well should be paid well and should be highly appreciated, especially those who work hard at both preaching and teaching" (1 Timothy 5:17, TLB).

God never intended His servants to exist at the level of bare subsistence, but many Christian workers have been distracted from their ministry by inadequate support. As someone has said "the poor and starving pastor should exist only among poor and starving people."

People ask us if we give only through our church. In our case, the answer is "no." However, giving to the local church that feeds you spiritually should be a priority. We give a minimum of 10 percent of our regular income through our church as a tangible expression of our commitment to it. But we also give to others who directly impact us. *"The one who is taught the Word is to share all good things with the one who teaches"* (Galatians 6:6).

2. Giving to the poor

Matthew 25:34-45 (NASB) teaches one of the most exciting and yet sobering truths in Scripture. Read this passage carefully.

"The King will say…'For I was hungry and you gave Me something to eat; I was thirsty, and you gave Me something to drink.'…Then the righteous will answer Him, 'Lord, when did we see You hungry, and feed You, or thirsty, and give You something to drink?'…The King will answer and say to them…'To the extent that you did it to one of these brothers of Mine, even the least of them, you did it to Me.' Then He will also say to those on His left, 'Depart from Me, accursed ones, into the eternal fire…for I was hungry, and you gave Me nothing to eat; I was thirsty, and you gave Me nothing to drink.…To the extent that you did not do it to one of the least of these, you did not do it to Me.'"

Jesus personally identifies Himself with the poor. When we share with the needy, we are actually sharing with Jesus Himself. If that truth is staggering, then this is terrifying – when we do not give to the needy, we leave Christ Himself hungry and thirsty.

During Christ's earthly ministry, He consistently gave to the poor. When Jesus told Judas to go and carry out the betrayal during the Last Supper *"no one at the meal understood why Jesus said this to him. Since Judas had charge of the money, some thought Jesus was telling him to buy what was needed for the Feast, or to give something to the poor"* (John 13:28-29).

Giving to the needy was such a consistent part of Jesus' life that the disciples assumed He was sending Judas either to buy needed food or to give to the poor; no other alternative entered their minds.

After Paul met with the disciples to announce his ministry to the Gentiles, he said *"they (the disciples) asked was that we should continue to remember the poor, the very thing I was eager to do"* (Galatians 2:10). Think of all the issues the disciples could have discussed with Paul. But the only request they made was to remember the poor. Now that should tell us something!

Three areas of our Christian life are affected by whether we give to the poor.

1. Prayer

A lack of giving to the poor could be a source of unanswered prayer. *"Is not this the kind of fasting I have chosen…to share your food with the hungry and to provide the poor wanderer with shelter.…Then you will call, and the Lord will answer"* (Isaiah 58:6-9). *"If a man shuts his ears to the cry of the poor, he too will cry out and not be answered"* (Proverbs 21:13).

2. Provision

Our giving to the needy may determine our provision. *"He who gives to the poor will not want, but he who hides his eyes will get many a curse"* (Proverbs 28:27, RSV).

3. Knowing Jesus Christ intimately

Those who do not share with the poor do not know God as intimately as they could: *"'He judged the cause of the poor and needy; then it was well. Was not this knowing Me?' says the Lord"* (Jeremiah 22:16, NKJV).

Giving to the poor has been discouraged, in part, because of government benefit programmes. God intended this to be the church's responsibility, not the government's.

Q: I thought the Bible says that if I give generously, God is supposed to prosper me. Why hasn't this happened? I'm confused.

A: It's important that you handle **all** your money God's way. Some people are generous, but suffer financially because they're dishonest or they don't work hard or they use credit to spend more than they can afford.

Q: Should we tithe to our local church?

A: In my opinion you should give at least 10 percent of your income to your church, and then give to other ministries and needs as God directs and provides.

The government often treats the needy impersonally and based on means testing. The church has the potential to be sensitive to their dignity. We can also develop one-on-one relationships to meet their immediate physical needs and then focus on their longer-term physical and spiritual needs. Mother Teresa is one of the best examples of someone who served the poor in a loving, compassionate way: she once said 'look after the poor…each one of them is Jesus in disguise.'

With household budgets stretched and consumerism having such a stranglehold, there often seems no place for giving to the poor. Nor should we assume that with the work of government agencies and the commitment of many excellent charities that the poor are provided for. It was always God's intention that his people should be responsible for helping the poor and around the country churches are doing just that. A friend's church supports a maternity hospital in Shyira, Rwanda and this initiative has received much support from the wider community. Other churches send practical support to Romania, support relief workers in Africa and much, much more. The passages just cited and the ministry of Jesus evidence that giving must include giving to the poor. The first instinct of Zacchaeus when he met Jesus was to put his financial dealings in order and to serve the poor.

Howard will often challenge people to pray that the Lord will bring one needy person into their lives. Could you give to a church programme that helps the poor? Should you give to a Christian agency that is supporting the poor through mission and relief work?

If you don't already know some needy people, please consider asking the Lord to include you in giving to the poor. You can do so by praying this prayer:

"Father God, by Your grace, create in me the desire to share with the needy. Bring me opportunities to give to the poor so that I might learn according to what pleases you."

This will be a significant step in maturing your relationship with Christ.

May we echo Job's statement: *"I delivered the poor who cried for help, and the orphan who had no helper.…I made the widow's heart sing for joy.…I was eyes to the blind and feet to the lame. I was a father to the needy, and I investigated the case which I did not know"* (Job 29:12-16, NASB).

Secular charities

Numerous secular charities (schools, community, organisations, charities that fight diseases) compete vigorously for our donations. Scripture does not address whether we should give to these charities. However, our family has decided not to make these organisations part of our regular giving. Our reason is that many people support secular charities, only those who know the Lord support the ministries of Christ. Do we apply this practice strictly? No, there are many times when we have given something from our pockets or notes from our wallet. Often this involves giving to someone we know who is seeking to work for a cause and we wish to encourage them for their commitment and willingness to serve charitable causes or we sense God's prompting to give.

> **Some of the most precious gifts that God gives are those that money can't buy and death can't steal**

module eight
My notes

What I learnt from studying giving:

What I plan to do differently:

My other notes:

> **"Steady plodding brings prosperity; hasty speculation brings poverty"**
> **(Proverbs 21:5, TLB)**

module nine
Investing

Consistently save

module nine
Personal study

To be completed **prior to** module nine meeting

Scripture to memorise
"Steady plodding brings prosperity; hasty speculation brings poverty"
(Proverbs 21:5, TLB)

Practical application
Complete a review of investment planning and look at your insurance options.

Day one – let's review giving
Read the giving notes on pages 108-115 and answer:

1. From God's perspective it is important to give with the proper attitude. How will this impact your giving?

2. What truth about giving did you learn that proved especially helpful? In what way?

Investing

Day two
Read Genesis 41:34-36; Proverbs 21:20 and Proverbs 30:24-25

1. What do these passages say to you about savings?

   Genesis 41:34-36:

Proverbs 21:20:

Proverbs 30:24-25:

2. If you are not yet saving, when and how do you propose to begin?

Read Luke 12:16-21, 34

3. Why did the Lord call the rich man a fool?

4. According to this parable, why do you think it is scripturally permissible to save only when you are also giving?

Day three
Read 1 Timothy 5:8

1. What is a scripturally acceptable reason for saving? What might this include?

Read 1 Timothy 6:9

2. What is a scripturally unacceptable reason for saving?

Read 1 Timothy 6:10

3. According to this verse, why is it wrong to want to get rich (refer to 1 Timothy 6:9)? Do you have the desire to get rich?

Read 1 Timothy 6:11

4. What should you do if you have the desire to get rich?

Day four
Read Proverbs 21:5; Proverbs 24:27; Proverbs 27:23-24; Ecclesiastes 3:1 and Ecclesiastes 11:2

1. What investment principle(s) can you learn from each of these verses, and how will you apply each principle to your life?

Proverbs 21:5:

Proverbs 24:27:

Proverbs 27:23-24:

Ecclesiastes 3:1:

Ecclesiastes 11:2:

Day five
Read Genesis 24:35-36; Proverbs 13:22 and 2 Corinthians 12:14

1. Should parents attempt to leave a material inheritance to their children? Why or why not?

2. How are you going to implement this principle?

Read Proverbs 20:21 and Galatians 4:1-2

3. What caution should a parent exercise?

Proverbs 20:21:

Galatians 4:1-2:

Day six

Gambling is defined as: *playing games of chance for money and betting.* Beware, gambling is often referred to as gaming. Some of today's most common forms of gambling include: online gambling, particularly online poker, sporting events, especially football, horse racing, day trading (in stocks and shares), the national lottery and its derivatives, scratch cards and casino gambling.

1. What are some of the motivations that cause people to gamble?

2. Why would these motives be displeasing to the Lord?

Read Proverbs 28:20 and Proverbs 28:22

3. According to these passages, why do you think a godly person should not gamble?

4. How does gambling contradict the scriptural principles of working diligently and being a faithful steward of the Lord's possessions?

☐ Please write your prayer requests in your prayer log before coming to the meeting.

module nine
Crown notes

To be read after completing **module nine** personal study

The Bible contains very practical investment advice. But before we take a look at what it says about investing, we need to be aware of two important principles.

Finding the balance: investing and giving

We need to balance our investing with generosity. Jesus told a parable of a farmer who harvested a bumper crop and said to himself *"'I have no place to store my crops....I will tear down my barns and build bigger ones, and there I will store all my grain and goods....' But God said to him, 'You fool!...This is how it will be with anyone who stores up things for himself but is not rich toward God....For where your treasure is, there your heart will be also'"* (Luke 12:16-21, 34, NASB).

The key word in this parable is *all*. Jesus called the farmer foolish because he saved everything. He didn't balance saving with giving. If we only pile up our investments, they will pull on our hearts like gravity. Our affection will be drawn away from God toward them because *"where your treasure is, there will your heart be also"* (Luke 12:34, KJV). However, if we give generously to God, we can invest and still love Him with all of our heart.

Danger ahead

Let's face it – most people want to have plenty of money. Let me refer to this as – getting rich – although this will be interpreted according to your own perspectives, similar to the newspaper snapshot we mentioned previously. I'll never forget how surprised I was the first time I saw how the Bible caution's against it: *"people who want to get rich fall into temptation and a trap and into many foolish and harmful desires that plunge men into ruin and destruction"* (1 Timothy 6:9). This verse says those who want to get rich give in to temptations and desires that ultimately lead to ruin. Wanting to get rich is accompanied by considerable risk, but why?

The next verse answers that question: *"for the love of money is a root of all kinds of evil. Some people, eager for money, have wandered from the faith and pierced themselves with many griefs"* (1 Timothy 6:10). When we want to get rich, we actually love money. That has consequences I witnessed firsthand. George became consumed by a desire to get rich. He finally abandoned his wife and two children and later denied Christ. He subsequently invested a sizeable proportion of his capital over in the USA only for the underlying investments to lose much of their value and the dollar weakened to the point where his overall wealth plummeted by over 50 percent.

The first step in investing is saving

What are the motivations for becoming rich? The obvious ones of financial security, independence and the ability to do as you please. Greed and pride also play a role as motivators. As a faithful steward, the motive changes when recognising that everything belongs to God and knowing that He will meet our needs. Our motive then, is to please Him with what He has entrusted to us. Our faith is in God's ability to provide and not in *our* wealth.

I am not saying it's wrong to become rich. Many heroes of the faith, such as Abraham and David, were rich. In fact, I rejoice when God enables a person who has been a faithful steward to prosper. Nothing is wrong with becoming wealthy if it is a by-product of being faithful.

Overcoming the temptation

You can overcome the temptation to get rich by remembering to split and submit! Paul told Timothy to *"flee from all this (the desire to get rich), and pursue righteousness, godliness, faith, love, endurance and gentleness"* (1 Timothy 6:11). When you become aware of a desire to get rich, run from it! Analyse what triggers your desire. I discovered a habit of dreaming about wealth when I would take a long look at my asset spreadsheet and imagine how much my investments might grow. I broke that mindset by adding a line at the end of the worksheet that read "belonging to God" – the formula was = – (line above). This means that my net worth is £ nil because even my spreadsheet is in line with Scripture.

The ultimate way of escape is submitting to God. We can do this confidently because Jesus overcame a huge temptation to become rich. After fasting 40 days, He was tempted three times by the devil. Here's the final temptation: *"the devil led him up to a high place and showed him in an instant all the kingdoms of the world. And he said to him, 'I will give you all their authority and splendour, for it has been given to me, and I can give it to anyone I want to. So if you worship me, it will all be yours'"* (Luke 4:5-7).

Jesus was offered all the kingdoms of the world. Because of His complete submission to His Father, He was empowered by the same Holy Spirit who lives in us to resist that temptation.

We believe that our heavenly Father does not usually allow His children to prosper when they are motivated to get rich. Wanting to get rich – loving money – closely parallels greed. And *"greed…amounts to idolatry"* (Colossians 3:5). It is for our sake that our Father protects us from loving anything that would draw us away from Him.

Saving

The first step in investing is saving. Unfortunately, most people are not consistent savers.

Look at this graph. It's shocking! We

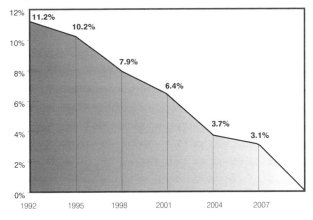

Source: Office of National Statistics

saved an average of 11.2 percent of our income in 1992. By 2007, our rate of saving had fallen to 3.1 percent, the lowest savings rate in the past 50 years!

The Bible, on the other hand, encourages us to save: *"the wise man saves for the future, but the foolish man spends whatever he gets"* (Proverbs 21:20, TLB). God commends the ant for saving *"there are four things which are little upon the earth, but they are exceeding wise. The ants are a people not strong, yet they prepare their meat in the summer"* (Proverbs 30:24-25). We need to think like ants! Even though they are small, they save. You may not be in a position to save a lot right now, but begin the habit.

Joseph saved during *"seven years of great abundance"* (Genesis 41:29) in order to survive during *"seven years of famine"* (Genesis 41:30). That is the purpose of saving; not spending today so that you will have something to spend in the future. Most people are poor savers because they don't see the value in practicing self-denial. Our culture screams that we deserve to get what we want, when we want it!

The most effective way to save is to make it automatic and regular. When you receive income, the first cheque or payment should be a gift to the Lord, and the second cheque should go to savings. An automatic bank transfer is a great way to save. Some people save their bonuses or a proportion of their overtime. Remember this: if you save immediately, you'll save more.

The Bible doesn't teach an amount to be saved. We recommend saving 10 percent of your income. This may not be possible initially. But begin the habit of saving – even if it's only a pound a month.

Emergency savings

Are your finances so finely balanced that if you had an unexpected cost you would not know how to pay for it other than on plastic or overdraft? If you do not have any emergency savings then start now. These savings will provide a cushion when an unexpected bill arises. Be careful and resist the temptation to raid these savings. How much to save? We recommend that you initially aim towards one week's income and then build this up to one month's income. It might take time to achieve – if you find it hard, start with some small steps, such as £5 a week. If you haven't been in the habit of saving – start now with your emergency savings.

Begin the habit of saving – even if it's only a pound a month

Understanding compound interest

A wealthy man was asked if he had seen the seven wonders of the world. He responded "No, but I do know the eighth wonder of the world – compounding." It's important to understand the three variables in compounding: the amount you save, the percentage rate you earn and the length of time you save.

1. The amount
The amount you save depends on your income and spending. We hope you will increase the amount available for saving as you learn God's way of handling money.

2. Rate of return
The second variable is the rate you earn on an investment. The following table demonstrates how an investment of £1,000 a year saved on a monthly basis grows at various rates.

Percent earned	Year 5	Year 10	Year 20	Year 30	Year 40
4%	5,502	12,222	30,442	57,606	98,102
6%	5,790	13,601	38,349	83,374	165,293
8%	6,098	15,184	48,888	123,669	289,753
10%	6,427	17,002	63,027	187,620	524,898

As you can see, an increase in rate has a remarkable effect on the amount accumulated. A 2 percent increase improves the return by approximately 75 per cent over 40 years. But since higher returns usually also carry higher risks, be careful not to shoot for unrealistic returns.

3. Time

Time is the third factor. Answer this: who would accumulate more by age 65: Jennifer who started saving £83.33 on a monthly basis (£1,000 per annum) at age 21, saved for eight years, and then completely stopped; or Matt who saved £83.33 on a monthly basis (£1,000 per annum) for 37 years starting at age 29? Both earned 6 percent. Is it Jennifer who saved a total of £8,000 or Matt who saved £37,000? Check out the following chart.

Age	Jennifer Contribution	Jennifer Year-end value	Matt Contribution	Matt Year-end value
21	1,000	1,124	0	0
22	1,000	2,111	0	0
23	1,000	3,265	0	0
24	1,000	4,490	0	0
25	1,000	5,790	0	0
26	1,000	7,172	0	0
27	1,000	8,638	0	0
28	1,000	10,195	0	0
29	0	10,806	1,000	1,124
30	0	11,455	1,000	2,111
31	0	12,142	1,000	3,265
32	0	12,870	1,000	4,490
33	0	13,643	1,000	5,790
34	0	14,461	1,000	7,171
35	0	15,329	1,000	8,638
36	0	16,249	1,000	10,195
37	0	17,224	1,000	11,847
38	0	18,257	1,000	13,602
39	0	19,353	1,000	15,464
40	0	20,514	1,000	17,442
41	0	21,745	1,000	19,542
42	0	23,049	1,000	21,771
43	0	24,432	1,000	24,137
44	0	25,898	1,000	26,650

45	0	27,452	1,000	29,318
46	0	29,100	1,000	32,150
47	0	30,846	1,000	35,157
48	0	32,696	1,000	38,349
49	0	34,658	1,000	41,738
50	0	36,738	1,000	45,336
51	0	38,942	1,000	49,156
52	0	41,278	1,000	53,212
53	0	43,755	1,000	57,518
54	0	46,380	1,000	62,089
55	0	49,162	1,000	66,943
56	0	52,112	1,000	72,096
57	0	55,239	1,000	77,566
58	0	58,553	1,000	83,374
59	0	62,066	1,000	89,540
60	0	65,790	1,000	96,087
61	0	69,734	1,000	103,037
62	0	73,921	1,000	110,416
63	0	78,356	1,000	118,250
64	0	83,058	1,000	126,568
65	0	**£88,041**	1,000	**£135,398**
Investment: £8,000			**£37,000**	

Jennifer only saved £8,000, but her total return was £88,041 while Matt saved £37,000 and saw a total return of £135,398. Jennifer received a gain of £80,041 while Matt's was £98,398, only £18,357 more. Interestingly, if the growth rate over the 37 years had averaged 10 percent, Jennifer would have actually accumulated more than Matt. The message? Start saving now!

Investing

People place some of their savings in investments in the hope of receiving an income or growth in value. The purpose of this Crown Financial Ministries study is not to recommend any specific investments. No one is authorised to use their affiliation with Crown to promote the sale of any investments or financial services. Our objective is to draw attention to the scriptural framework for savings and investing.

1. Be a steady plodder

The fundamental principle for becoming a successful investor is to spend less than you earn and regularly invest the surplus. In other words, be a steady plodder. The Bible says *"steady plodding brings prosperity, hasty speculation brings poverty"* (Proverbs 21:5, TLB). The original words for 'steady plodding' picture a person filling a large barrel one handful at a time. Little by little the barrel is filled. Nothing replaces consistent, month-on-month saving.

2. Avoid risky investments

God warns us to avoid risky investments, yet each year thousands of people lose money in highly speculative investments and scams. The Bible says *"there is another serious problem I have seen everywhere – savings are put into risky investments that turn sour, and soon there is nothing left to pass on to one's son. The man who speculates is soon back to where he began – with nothing"* (Ecclesiastes 5:13-15, TLB).

How many times have you heard of people losing their life's savings on a get-rich-quick scheme? Sadly, it seems that Christians are particularly vulnerable because they trust others who appear to live by their same values. The strategy for avoiding risky investments is to pray, seek wise counsel and do your homework.

3. Diversify

Money can be lost on any investment. Stocks and shares, investments bonds, unit trusts, freehold property where the capital and income can be at risk or deposit accounts, where normally only a certain amount of the capital is 100 percent secure and interest returns fluctuate. They can all perform well or poorly. Each investment has its own advantages and disadvantages. Since the perfect investment doesn't exist, we need to diversify and not put all our eggs in one basket. *"Divide your portion to seven, or even to eight, for you do not know what misfortune may occur on the earth"* (Ecclesiastes 11:2, NASB).

4. Count the cost

Every investment has costs: financial, time, effort and sometimes even emotional stress. For example, a rental property will require time and effort to rent and maintain. If the tenant is irresponsible, you may have to try to collect rent from someone who doesn't want to pay – talk about emotions! Before you decide on any investment, consider all the costs.

What God wants a successful investor to do

God understands that when we increase our assets, they can become a potential barrier to an intimate relationship with Him. If you have a lot of resources, the Lord isn't disappointed or surprised; rather He entrusted it to you for a purpose. In 1 Timothy 6:17-19, God gives us instructions to help those with resources to remain undistracted from loving Him.

1. Do not be conceited

"Instruct those who are rich (successful investors) in this present world not to be conceited" (1 Timothy 6:17, NASB). Wealth tends to produce pride. Howard Dayton tells how for several years he drove two vehicles. The first was an old pickup truck. When he drove that truck to the bank drive-in window to cash a cheque, he was humble. Howard knew the cashier was going to carefully check his account to confirm that the driver of that beat-up truck had sufficient funds in his account. And when he received the money, he drove away with a song in his heart and praises on his lips.

His other vehicle was a well-preserved, second-hand car that was expensive when it was new. When he drove that car to the bank, he appeared to be a different person. He was a person who deserved a certain amount of respect. Howard wasn't quite as patient when the cashier examined his account, and when he received the money he was not as grateful. Wealth often leads to pride.

Your questions

Q: I'm 55 years old. Is it too late for me to begin to save and invest?

A: Absolutely not! It's never too late to begin to apply God's financial principles. The key is simply to be faithful starting today.

Q: I like investing in high-risk, high-return investments. Unfortunately, my wife does not feel comfortable with my approach. How can I convince her I'm right?

A: Listen to her advice! God speaks most clearly to the husband through his wife.

2. Put no confidence in your assets

"Instruct those who are rich in this present world not…to fix their hope on the uncertainty of riches, but on God, who richly supplies us with all things to enjoy" (1 Timothy 6:17, NASB).

The ability to accumulate assets without placing our confidence in them is a struggle. We tend to trust in the seen rather than in the invisible living God. It is easy to trust in money, because money can buy things. But we need to remind ourselves that possessions can be lost and that God alone can be fully trusted.

3. Give generously

"Instruct them to do good, to be rich in good works, to be generous and ready to share, storing up for themselves the treasure of a good foundation for the future, so that they may take hold of that which is life indeed" (1 Timothy 6:18-19, NASB). The Lord wants successful investors to be generous and tells them of two benefits: (1) eternal treasures that they will enjoy forever, and (2) the blessing of "taking hold of that which is life indeed." By exercising generosity, they can live the fulfilling life God intends for them now.

> **We should never participate in gambling/gaming or lotteries – not even for entertainment**

Other issues

Gambling/gaming and lotteries

Lotteries and gambling of all types are endemic in this country. Internet gambling continues to grow exponentially. Approximately 70 percent of the adult population gambles whether it is online gaming or the lottery.

As this is now a £40 billion industry and over 2,000 websites are available to gamble online, the average adult gambles more than £1,000 a year. In many cases this is more than is saved and certainly greater than anything given. There is no greater gap between the world's economy and God's economy. The chances of winning are more than remote and so money spent in this manner, is, I certainly regard, fleshy and wasteful.

Sadly, more than 30 million are addicted to gambling, with consequences that are heartbreaking for their loved ones. Although the Bible does not specifically prohibit gambling, it's the *get-rich-quick* motivation that violates the steady plodding principle.

In my opinion, we should *never* participate in gambling or lotteries – even for entertainment. We should not expose ourselves to the risk of becoming compulsive gamblers, nor should we support an industry that enslaves so many.

Inheritance

> **It is important to prepare financially for your death**

Parents should try to leave an inheritance for their children: *"A good man leaves an inheritance to his children's children"* (Proverbs 13:22, NASB). But inheritances should not be dispensed until heirs have been trained to be wise stewards. *"An inheritance quickly gained at the beginning will not be blessed at the end"* (Proverbs 20:21). Consider making distributions over several years, as heirs mature enough to handle the responsibility of money. Select trustworthy people to help supervise the finances of young heirs until they are capable stewards. *"As long as the heir is a child, he is no different from a slave, although he owns the whole estate. He is subject to guardians and trustees until the time set by his father"* (Galatians 4:1-2).

Wills

It is important to prepare financially for your death. As Isaiah told Hezekiah *"this is what the Lord says: 'Put your house in order, because you are going to die; you will not recover'"* (2 Kings 20:1). One of the greatest gifts you can leave your loved ones for that emotional time is an organised estate and a properly prepared Will. If you don't have a current Will, make an appointment this week with a solicitor to prepare one.

The one guaranteed investment

I was 12 years old when I was introduced to the only guaranteed investment. I attended a Christian youth camp in Criccieth, North Wales. I attended the evening camp meetings and listened to the camp evangelist and recognised that I needed Jesus Christ as my Saviour, and, as He had invested His life for me, I should accept His sacrifice and ask Him to forgive my sin and be part of my life.

God loves you and wants you to know Him

God created people in His own image, and He desires an intimate relationship with each of us. *"For God so loved the world, that he gave his only begotten Son, that whosoever believeth in him should not perish, but have everlasting life"* (John 3:16, KJV). We also read that *"I (Jesus) has come that they may have life, and have it to the full"* (John 10:10).

We are separated from God

God is holy. This means God is perfect, and He will not have a relationship with anyone who also is not perfect. *"For all have sinned and fall short of the glory of God"* (Romans 3:23). Sin separates us from God: *"Your sins have cut you off from God"* (Isaiah 59:2, TLB).

The diagram illustrates our separation from God. An enormous gap separates us from God. Individuals try without success to bridge this gap through their own efforts, such as living a good, moral life or doing good deeds.

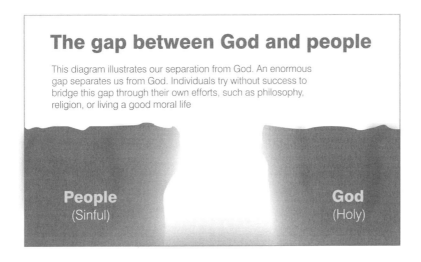

The gap between God and people

This diagram illustrates our separation from God. An enormous gap separates us from God. Individuals try without success to bridge this gap through their own efforts, such as philosophy, religion, or living a good moral life

People
(Sinful)

God
(Holy)

God's only provision to bridge this gap: Jesus Christ

Jesus Christ died on the cross to pay the penalty for our sin and bridge the gap between us and God. Jesus said: *"I am the way, the truth, and the life: no man cometh unto the Father, but by me"* (John 14:6, KJV). *"But God demonstrates His own love toward us, in that while we were yet sinners, Christ died for us"* (Romans 5:8, NKJV).

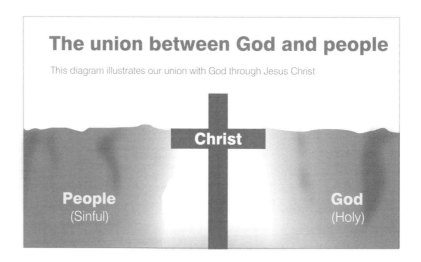

This relationship is a gift from God

As an act of faith you can also receive the free gift of a life with an eternal relationship with God. Free? Yes. *"For by grace you have been saved through faith; and this is not your own doing, it is the gift of God – not because of works, lest any man should boast"* (Ephesians 2:8-9, RSV).

We must all receive Jesus Christ individually

At the age of twelve I had only to turn away (repent of) my sins and ask Jesus Christ to come into my life and become my Saviour and Lord. And I did.

After more than forty years as a Christian, I can confirm beyond a shadow of doubt that a relationship with God can be yours through Jesus Christ. Nothing I know compares with the privilege of knowing Christ personally.

If you desire to know the Lord and are not certain whether you have this relationship, I encourage you to ask Christ to come into your life by saying this prayer:

Father God, I need you I admit I have done wrong and I want to turn away from that life. I invite you, Jesus, to come into my life and make me the person You want me to be. Thank you for forgiving my sins and giving me the gift of eternal life.

You might fulfil each of the principles in becoming a faithful steward, but without a relationship with Christ, your efforts will be in vain. If you asked Christ into your life, begin to attend a church that teaches the Bible so that you can learn and mature in your faith.

module nine
My notes

What I learnt from studying investing:

What I plan to do differently:

My other notes:

module nine
My notes

> "For what will it profit a man if he gains the whole world, and loses his own soul?"
> (Mark 8:36, NKJV)

module ten
Eternity

All will give an account

module ten
Personal study

To be completed **prior to** module ten meeting

Scripture to memorise
"For what will it profit a man if he gains the whole world, and loses his own soul?"
(Mark 8:36, NKJV)

Practical application
Complete 'my life goals.' Also, complete the involvement and suggestions survey in the small group section of Crownuk.org.

Day one – let's review investing
Read the investing notes on pages 122-130 and answer:

1. What in the notes, did you find most useful?

2. Describe the steps you intend to take?

Eternity

Day two
Read Psalm 39:4-6 and Psalm 103:13-16

1. What do these passages say to you about the length of life on earth?

Read Psalm 90:10, 12

2. Why did Moses ask God to teach us to number our days?

3. Estimate the number of days you have left on earth. How does this impact your thinking?

4. Based on your number of days, what, if anything, will you do differently?

Day three
Read 1 Chronicles 29:15; Philippians 3:20 and 1 Peter 2:11

1. What do these passages say about your identity on earth and in heaven?

   1 Chronicles 29:15:

   Philippians 3:20:

   1 Peter 2:11:

Read 2 Peter 3:10-13

2. What will happen to the earth?

3. How should this impact the way you invest your time and spend money?

Day four
Read Ecclesiastes 12:13-14 and 2 Corinthians 5:9-10

1. What will happen to each of us in the future?

    Ecclesiastes 12:13-14:

    2 Corinthians 5:9-10:

Read 1 Corinthians 3:11-15

2. How would you describe the works (give some examples) that will be burned at this final judgement?

3. Give some examples of works that will be rewarded.

4. What are you doing that will survive this final judgement?

Day five
Read 2 Corinthians 4:18

1. What does this verse say to you?

2. As you reflect on eternity, answer this question thoughtfully: what three things do I want to accomplish during the rest of my life? How will you move to achieve these goals?

3. What can I do during my lifetime that would contribute most significantly to the cause of Christ?

4. What will I do in the next three months towards this cause?

5. In light of these answers, what actions or changes do I need to make?

Day six
Read the eternity notes on pages 138-144 and answer:

1. What was the most important concept you learned from reading the notes?

2. If you have access to the Internet please complete the Involvement and Suggestions Survey in the My Crown section of Crownuk.org.

3. Describe what has been the most beneficial part of the *Biblical Financial Study* for you:

☐ **Please write your prayer requests in your prayer log before coming to the meeting.**

module ten
Crown notes

To be read after completing **module ten** personal study

On Monday, October 25, 1999, the news reported an unfolding story. Air Force jets following a Lear jet from Orlando, Florida, were unable to communicate with its pilots. Howard learned later that two very close friends, Robert Fraley and Van Ardan, were on that Lear as it carried them and golfer Payne Stewart to their deaths.

One of the most critical principles for us to understand when handling money is the reality of eternity. Robert and Van were men in their mid-forties who lived with an eternal perspective. Robert had these words framed in his gym "take care of your body as though you will live forever; take care of your soul as if you will die tomorrow."

Because God loves us, He reveals in the Bible that there is a heaven and a hell, that there is a coming judgement, and that He will grant eternal rewards. The Lord wants the very best for us. Therefore, He wants to motivate us to invest our lives and finances in such a way that we can enjoy an intimate relationship with Him now and receive the greatest possible rewards and responsibilities in heaven.

Our failure to view our present lives through the lens of eternity is one of the biggest hindrances to seeing our lives and our finances in their true light. Yet Scripture states that the reality of our eternal future should determine the character of our present lives and the use of our money and possessions.

People who do not know the Lord look at life as a brief interval that begins at birth and ends at death. Looking to the future, they see no further than their own life span. With no eternal perspective, they think if this life is all there is why deny myself any pleasure or possession?

Those who know Christ have an entirely different perspective. We know life is short; it is the preface – not the book; it is the preliminary scene – not the main event. This testing period will determine much of our experience in heaven.

Financial planners try to convince people to look down the road instead of simply focusing on today. "Don't think in terms of this year," they will tell you. "Think and plan for 30 years from now." The wise person does indeed think ahead, but far more than 30 years – 30 thousand years and more ahead. Someone once said "he who provides for this life but takes no care for eternity is wise for a moment but a fool forever." Jesus said it this way, *"what good is it for a man to gain the whole world, yet forfeit his soul?"* (Mark 8:36).

Earthly goods will not last forever – they are destined for annihilation

The long and short of it

The Bible frequently reminds us that life on earth is brief: *"for He knows our frame; He remembers that we are dust"* (Psalm 103:14, NKJV). If you live for 70 years your life will comprise of just over 600,000 hours. Our earthly bodies are called 'tents' (2 Peter 1:13), temporary dwelling places of our eternal souls. David recognised this and sought to gain God's perspective on the brevity of life. He asked of God *"show me, O Lord, my life's end and the number of my days; let me know how fleeting is my life. You have made my days a mere handbreadth; the span of my years is as nothing before you. Each man's life is but a breath. Man is a mere phantom…he heaps up wealth, not knowing who will get it"* (Psalm 39:4-6).

When a good friend discovered she had only a short time to live, she told me of her radical change in perspective. "The most striking thing that's happened," she said "is that I find myself almost totally uninterested in accumulating more things. Things used to matter to me, but now I find my thoughts are centered on Christ, my friends and other people."

Moses realised that true wisdom flowed out of understanding that our lives are short. So he asked the Lord to help him number the days he had on earth. *"the length of our days is seventy years – or eighty, if we have the strength…for they quickly pass, and we fly away…So teach us to number our days aright, that we may gain a heart of wisdom"* (Psalm 90:10, 12).

I encourage you to number the days you estimate that you have left on earth. If I live as long as my father, I have about 12,000 days left. This has helped me become aware that I need to invest my life and resources in eternally important matters.

When we lived in Bristol, we were totally immersed in church and social life. Bristol was our home for over twenty years. Then we decided to move to Bath and our complete focus changed to starting a new life, new neighbours, new friends and new church. In a similar way, we should remember that we are 'here today, gone tomorrow' – from earth, our temporary home, to our real home in heaven. Having been involved in three accidents, each one of which could easily have killed me, I am thankful for every day here on this earth, but know one day where I'm going. Do we live every day as though it were our last? God had given us life through his Son, we should share it with as many people as possible – being in eternity will bear no resemblance to our time here on this earth.

> "It ought to be the business of every day to prepare for our last day."
>
> **Matthew Henry**

Eternity is long – very long!

Eternity, on the other hand, never ends. It is forever. Imagine a cable running through the room where you are now. To your right, the cable runs millions of light years all the way to the end of the universe; to your left, it runs to the other end of the universe. Now imagine that the cable to your left represents eternity past, and the cable to your right, eternity future. Place a small mark on the cable in front of you; the mark represents your brief life on earth.

Because most people do not have an eternal perspective, they live as if the mark were all there is. They make mark choices, living in mark houses, driving mark cars, wearing mark clothes, and raising mark children. One author referred to eternity as 'the long tomorrow.' This is the backdrop against which all the questions of life and the handling of our resources must be answered.

Aliens and pilgrims

Scripture tells us several things about our identity and role on earth. First *"our citizenship is in heaven,"* (Philippians 3:20) not earth. Second, *"we are ambassadors for Christ,"* (2 Corinthians 5:20), representing Him on earth. Imagine yourself as an ambassador working in a country that is generally hostile to your own. Naturally, you want to learn about this new place, see the sights and become familiar with the people and culture. But suppose you eventually become so assimilated into this foreign country that you begin to regard it as your true home. Your allegiance wavers, and you gradually compromise your position as an ambassador, becoming increasingly ineffective in representing the best interests of your own country.

We must never become too much at home in this world or we will become ineffective in serving the cause of the Kingdom we are here to represent. We are aliens, strangers and pilgrims on earth. Peter wrote *"live your lives as strangers here in reverent fear"* (1 Peter 1:17). Later he added *"I urge you, as aliens and strangers in the world, to abstain from sinful desires"* (1 Peter 2:11, KJV).

Pilgrims are unattached. They are travellers – not settlers – aware that the excessive accumulation of things can distract. Material things are valuable to pilgrims but only as they facilitate their mission. Things can entrench us in the present world, acting as chains around our legs that keep us from moving in response to God. When our eyes are too focused on the visible, they will be drawn away from the invisible. *"O we fix our eyes not on what is seen, but on what is unseen. For what is seen is temporary, but what is unseen is eternal"* (2 Corinthians 4:18).

Pilgrims of faith look to the next world. They see earthly possessions for what they are: useful for Kingdom purposes, but far too flimsy to bear the weight of trust. 'Let temporal things serve your use, but the eternal be the object of your desire.' Two principles concerning possessions help us gain a proper perspective of them.

1. We leave it all behind

I acted as an executor for a distinguished businessman who had enjoyed success and a meteoric career. I was approached one day by the two children who asked me how much Dad had left. 'All of it,' was the reply. No trailer ever follows a hearse, 'he left it all.' Job said it this way, *"naked I came from my mother's womb, and naked I shall depart"* (Job 1:21). Paul wrote, *"we brought nothing into the world, and we can take nothing out of it"* (1 Timothy 6:7).

The psalmist observed *"do not be overawed when a man grows rich…for he will take nothing with him when he dies, his splendour will not descend with him. Though while he lived he counted himself blessed – and men praise you when you prosper – he will join the generation of his fathers, who will never see the light of life"* (Psalm 49:16-19).

2. Everything will be destroyed

Earthly goods will not last forever – they are destined for annihilation. *"But the day of the Lord will come as a thief in the night; in which the heavens shall pass away with a great noise, and the elements shall melt with fervent heat, the earth also and the works that are therein shall be burned up. Seeing then that all these things shall be dissolved, what manner of persons ought you to be in all holy conversation and godliness?"* (2 Peter 3:10-11, KJV). Understanding the temporary nature of possessions should influence us as we consider spending decisions.

Judgement

It is uncomfortable to think about judgement. But because our Lord loves us so deeply, He wants us to realise what will happen in the future. Therefore, God revealed to us that we will all be judged according to our deeds: *"He has appointed a day on which He will judge the world in righteousness"* (Acts 17:31, NKJV). All of us should live each day with this awareness: *"they will give an account to Him who is ready to judge the living and the dead"* (1 Peter 4:5, NKJV).

God will judge us with total knowledge: *"nothing in all creation is hidden from God's sight. Everything is uncovered and laid bare before the eyes of him to whom we must give account"* (Hebrews 4:13). Because His knowledge is total, his judgement is comprehensive: *"men will have to give account on the day of judgement for every careless word they have spoken"* (Matthew 12:36). His judgement extends to what is hidden from people. *"For God will bring every deed into judgement, including every hidden thing, whether it is good or evil"* (Ecclesiastes 12:14). He will even *"disclose the motives of men's hearts"* (1 Corinthians 4:5).

The Bible teaches that all those who do not know Christ will be judged and sent to an indescribably dreadful place. *"I saw a great white throne and him who was seated on it…and I saw the dead, great and small, standing before the throne…each person was judged according to what he had done.…If anyone's name was not found written in the book of life, he was thrown into the lake of fire"* (Revelation 20:11-15).

Judgment of believers

After they die, those who know Christ will spend eternity with God in heaven, an incredibly wonderful place. But what we seldom consider is that the entry point to heaven is a judgement.

Scripture teaches that all believers in Christ will give an account of their lives to the Lord. *"We will all stand before God's judgement seat. So then, each of us will give an account of himself to God "* (Romans 14:10, 12). The result of this will be the gain or loss of eternal rewards. In 1 Corinthians 3:13-15 we read *"His work will be shown for what it is, because the (Judgement) Day will bring it to light.…If what he has built survives, he will receive his reward. If it is burned up, he will suffer loss."* Our works are what we have done with our time, influence, talents and resources. God's Word does not treat this judgement as just a meaningless formality before we get on to the real business of heaven. Rather Scripture presents it as a monumental event in which things of eternal significance are brought to light.

> **Everyone will have to give an account of their lives to the Lord**

Motivation and rewards

Why should I follow God's guidance on money and possessions when it is so much fun to do whatever I please with my resources? I'm a Christian. I know I'm going to heaven anyway. Why not have the best of both worlds — this one and the next? Though few of us would be honest enough to use such language, these questions reflect a common attitude.

The prospect of eternal rewards for our obedience is a neglected key to unlocking our motivation. Paul was motivated by the prospect of eternal rewards. He wrote *"I have fought the good fight, I have finished the race, I have kept the faith. Now there is in store for me the crown of righteousness, which the Lord, the righteous Judge, will award to me on that day – and not only to me, but also to all who have longed for his appearing"* (2 Timothy 4:7-8). God appeals not only to our compassion but also to our eternal self-interest. *"Love your enemies, and do good, and lend, expecting nothing in return; and your reward will be great"* (Luke 6:35, RSV).

Our heavenly Father uses three things to motivate us to obey Him: the love of God, the fear of God and the rewards of God. These are the same things that motivated my children to obey me. Sometimes their love for me was sufficient motivation, but other times it wasn't. In a healthy sense, they also feared me. They knew I would discipline them

> **Your questions**
>
> **Q:** Why is it important to write down my financial goals?
>
> **A:** Writing down your goals is powerful because it helps you clarify your thinking, monitor your progress and make midcourse corrections.

for wrongdoing. They also knew I would reward them with my words of approval and sometimes in tangible ways for doing right.

Unequal rewards in heaven

It is not as simple as saying "I'll be in heaven and that's all that matters." On the contrary, Paul spoke about the loss of reward as a terrible loss. The receiving of rewards from Christ is a phenomenal gain. Not all Christians will have the same rewards in heaven.

John Wesley said "I value all things only by the price they shall gain in eternity." God's kingdom was the reference point for him. He lived as he did, not because he did not treasure things, but because he treasured the right things. We often miss something in missionary martyr Jim Elliot's words "he is no fool who gives what he cannot keep to gain what he cannot lose." If we focus on Elliot's willingness to sacrifice, we overlook his motivation for gain. What separated him from many Christians was not that he didn't want treasure but that he wanted real treasure. Remember God loves you deeply. Because He wants the best for you throughout eternity, God has revealed that today's financial sacrifices and service for Him will pay off forever.

Impacting eternity today

Our daily choices determine what will happen in the future. What we do in this life is of eternal importance. We only live on this earth once *"just as man is destined to die once, and after that to face judgement"* (Hebrews 9:27). There is no such thing as reincarnation. Once our life on earth is over, we will never have another chance to move the hand of God through prayer, to share Christ with one who does not know the Saviour, to give money to further God's kingdom or to share with the needy.

Those who dabble in photography understand the effect of the 'fixer.' In developing a photograph, the negatives are immersed in several different solutions. The developing solution parallels this life. As long as the photograph is in the developing solution, it is subject to change. But when it is dropped in the fixer or 'stop bath,' it is permanently fixed, and the photograph is developed. So it will be when we enter eternity: the life each of us lives on earth will be fixed, never to be altered or revised.

Alfred Nobel was a Swedish chemist who made a fortune by inventing dynamite and explosives for weapons. When Nobel's brother died, a newspaper accidentally printed Alfred's obituary instead. He was described as a man who became rich by enabling people to kill each other with powerful weapons. Shaken from this assessment, Nobel resolved to use his fortune to reward accomplishments that benefit humanity. We now know those rewards as the Nobel Peace Prize. Let us put ourselves in Nobel's place. Let us read our own obituary, not as written by people but as it would be written from heaven's point of view. Then let us use the rest of our lives to edit that obituary into what we really want it to be.

As a little boy I used to stay with my grandmother in Rainhill, Liverpool. Every summer I would make friends and play at the recreation ground. I used to rush over to the edge of the 'rec' to watch the steam trains pass by before resuming my games. I spent weeks and weeks making up games and playing all over the grounds. Then one day, my gran passed away and it was another 20 years before I revisited the rec. I was so surprised, for it all looked so small. I could actually walk around it in less than four minutes. Many of those things that seem so large and important to us today, shrink into insignificance in just a few years.

When I am face to face with Christ and look back on my life, I want to see that the things in which I invested my time, creativity, influence and money are big things to Him. I do not want to squander my life on things that will not matter throughout eternity.

During Moses' time, Pharaoh was the most powerful person on earth. Pharaoh's daughter adopted Moses as an infant, giving him the opportunity to enjoy the wealth and prestige of a member of the royal family. Hebrews 11:24-26 tells us what Moses later chose and why. *"by faith Moses, when he had grown up, refused to be known as the son of Pharaoh's daughter. He chose to be ill-treated along with the people of God rather than to enjoy the pleasures of sin for a short time. He regarded disgrace for the sake of Christ as of greater value than the treasures of Egypt, because he was looking ahead to his reward."* Because Moses was looking forward to the only rewards that would last, he chose to identify with his people, the Hebrews, rather than the Egyptians and was used by God in a remarkable way.

What are the choices facing you now? How does an eternal perspective influence your decisions? Martin Luther said his calendar consisted of only two days: 'today' and 'that Day.' May we invest all that we are and have today in light of that day.

Let's review

At the beginning of this study, we asked why the Bible says so much about money and possessions — in more than 2,350 verses. We offered four reasons:

1. How we handle money impacts our fellowship with God
2. Money is the primary competitor with Christ for the Lordship of our life
3. Money moulds our character
4. The Lord wants us to have a road map for handling money so that we can become financially faithful in very practical ways

Review this diagram of the wheel, identifying the eight areas of our responsibilities, each with its primary thrust.

Faithfulness is a journey

Applying the financial principles of the Bible is a journey that takes time. It's easy to become discouraged if your finances aren't completely under control at the end of this study. Don't be discouraged, it takes the average person at least a year to apply most of these principles, and even longer if you have made financial mistakes. Many graduates of this course decide to lead this study because they know the leaders learn more than anyone else. As they help their Crown study members, the leaders make progress on their own journey to true financial freedom.

Faithfulness in small matters is foundational

Some people become frustrated by the inability to solve their financial problems quickly. Remember, simply be faithful with what you have — whether it is little or much. Some abandon the goal of becoming debt free or increasing their savings or giving because the task looks impossible. And perhaps it is — without God's help. Your job is to make a genuine effort, no matter how small it may appear, and then leave the results to God. I love what God said to the prophet Zechariah *"for who has despised the day of small things?"* (Zechariah 4:10, NASB). Don't be discouraged. Be persistent. Be faithful in even the smallest matters. We have repeatedly seen God bless those who tried to be faithful.

Now is the time!

We are not economists, but in leading Crown we know that God has equipped us with experience in understanding and applying the biblical principles you are studying. The first half of the twenty first century, has seen very challenging and difficult financial times. Tough times pass and good times return – that is the lesson we learn from studying past economic cycles. In applying the principles you have studied you will be laying a secure foundation for this life and the life to come. You have a window of opportunity to conform to His Word in the area of your money, wealth and possessions. We strongly encourage you to seize the moment and the opportunity. Become diligent in your efforts to get out of debt, give generously, stick to a spending plan and work as unto the Lord. In short, become a faithful steward.

Now that you know the biblical framework for managing money, you have half of the solution. The other half is that you must apply what you have learned. Jesus said *"therefore whoever hears these sayings of Mine, and does them, I will liken him to a wise man who built his house on the rock: and the rain descended, the floods came, and the winds blew and beat on that house; and it did not fall, for it was founded on the rock. But everyone who hears these sayings of Mine, and does not do them, will be like a foolish man who built his house on the sand: and the rain descended, the floods came, and the winds blew and beat on that house; and it fell. And great was its fall"* (Matthew 7:24-27, NKJV).

Economic times are already very tough. If you have acted and built your house upon the rock-solid principles of Scripture, your house will not fall. One of the best ways to demonstrate your love for your family and friends is to get your financial house in order and encourage others to do the same.

If you have a desire to help others learn God's way of handling money we encourage you to serve in one of the following ways:

- You may serve individuals as a Crown study group leader
- If one does not exist, would you be able to serve as a church coordinator or be on the church's Crown team? This is an opportunity to serve the church
- Maybe you have a desire to reach the community in starting or serving on a city team. Larger cities or counties require an area coordinator and team of volunteers
- Finally, if you have a 'missionary' spirit you may wish to help introduce Crown to other cities

For all of these opportunities we would be pleased to work with you and the church leadership. Please tell your leader if you wish to become a leader or co-leader or to serve on your church team. If you wish to serve your entire city or county, contact Crown Financial Ministries – see www.crownuk.org: Contact us. We appreciate the effort you have invested in this study. And we pray this has given you a greater appreciation for the Bible, helped you develop close friendships, and above all, nurtured your love for Jesus Christ. May God richly bless you on your journey to true financial freedom.

"When we've been there ten thousand years,
Bright shining as the sun,
We've no less days to sing God's praise
Than when we've first begun."

John P. Rees, Stanza 5, *Amazing Grace*

module ten
My notes

What I learnt from studying eternity:

What I plan to do differently:

My other notes:

"Pray for one another....The effective prayer of a righteous man can accomplish much"
(James 5:16)

always pray
Prayer logs

Be faithful in prayer

"Pray for one another" James 5:16

Name	Spouse
Home phone	Children (ages)
Business phone	
Mobile	
Email	
Address	

Week	Prayer request(s)	Answers to prayer
1	CAROL ✓	SELL HOUSE.
2	COLIN.	CONTINUE WITH WALK OF GOD NEXT STAGE.
3	JOGESH	PERMANENT OFFER OF EMPLOYMENT.
4	GILL.	HOUSE IN SPAIN TO SELL.
5	JOGESH	WISDOM FROM GOD.
6	TIM	EYE MIGRANES.
7	TINA	ANSWERS TO PRAYER
8	CHURCH.	FINANCES TO COME IN.
9		
10	Long-term prayer request:	

"Pray for one another" James 5:16

Name _____

Home phone _____

Business phone _____

Mobile _____

Email _____

Address _____

_____

Spouse _____

Children (ages) _____

_____

_____

_____

_____

Week	Prayer request(s)	Answers to prayer
1		
2		
3		
4		
5		
6		
7		
8		
9		
10	Long-term prayer request:	

"Pray for one another" James 5:16

Name _____

Home phone _____

Business phone _____

Mobile _____

Email _____

Address _____

_____

Spouse _____

Children (ages) _____

_____

_____

_____

_____

_____

Week	Prayer request(s)	Answers to prayer
1		
2		
3		
4		
5		
6		
7		
8		
9		
10	Long-term prayer request:	

"Pray for one another" James 5:16

Name _____

Home phone _____

Business phone _____

Mobile _____

Email _____

Address _____

_____

Spouse _____

Children (ages) _____

_____

_____

_____

_____

_____

Week	Prayer request(s)	Answers to prayer
1		
2		
3		
4		
5		
6		
7		
8		
9		
10	Long-term prayer request:	

"Pray for one another" James 5:16

Name _____

Home phone _____

Business phone _____

Mobile _____

Email _____

Address _____

_____

Spouse _____

Children (ages) _____

_____

_____

_____

_____

Week	Prayer request(s)	Answers to prayer
1		
2		
3		
4		
5		
6		
7		
8		
9		
10	Long-term prayer request:	

"Pray for one another" James 5:16

Name _____

Home phone _____

Business phone _____

Mobile _____

Email _____

Address _____

_____

Spouse _____

Children (ages) _____

_____

_____

_____

_____

_____

Week	Prayer request(s)	Answers to prayer
1		
2		
3		
4		
5		
6		
7		
8		
9		
10	Long-term prayer request:	

"Pray for one another" James 5:16

Name _____

Home phone _____

Business phone _____

Mobile _____

Email _____

Address _____

_____

Spouse _____

Children (ages) _____

_____

_____

_____

_____

Week	Prayer request(s)	Answers to prayer
1		
2		
3		
4		
5		
6		
7		
8		
9		
10	Long-term prayer request:	

"Pray for one another" James 5:16

Name	Spouse
Home phone	Children (ages)
Business phone	
Mobile	
Email	
Address	

Week	Prayer request(s)	Answers to prayer
1		
2		
3		
4		
5		
6		
7		
8		
9		
10	Long-term prayer request:	

"Pray for one another" James 5:16

Name	Spouse
Home phone	Children (ages)
Business phone	
Mobile	
Email	
Address	

Week	Prayer request(s)	Answers to prayer
1		
2		
3		
4		
5		
6		
7		
8		
9		
10	Long-term prayer request:	

"Pray for one another" James 5:16

Name _____

Home phone _____

Business phone _____

Mobile _____

Email _____

Address _____

_____

Spouse _____

Children (ages) _____

_____

_____

_____

_____

_____

Week	Prayer request(s)	Answers to prayer
1		
2		
3		
4		
5		
6		
7		
8		
9		
10	Long-term prayer request:	